ANATOLIA AND
ITS BIBLICAL VISIONARIES

ANATOLIA AND ITS BIBLICAL VISIONARIES

Anna G. Edmonds

ARCHAEOLOGY & ART PUBLICATIONS

ARCHAEOLOGY & ART PUBLICATIONS
ANATOLIA AND
ITS BIBLICAL VISIONARIES
Anna G. Edmonds

Publisher
Nezih Başgelen

Editor
Brian Johnson

Designer
Lalehan Uysal

Typesetter
Emel Yaşkabak

Printed By
Altan Matbaacılık
2002, Istanbul

ISBN 975-6561-24-6
Copyright text: © Anna G. Edmonds, 2002

First published in 2002 by Archaeology and Art Publications
Hayriye Cad., Çorlu Apt. 3/4, Galatasaray, Istanbul, Turkey 80060
www.arkeolojisanat.com

Front cover illustration: Old Testament kings and prophets,
Gülşehir, Cappadocia

CONTENTS

PREFACE

For ages on ages, Turkey has been a land where seers have seen visions and prophets have spoken prophesies. The country, or more precisely the Asiatic portion of it known today as Anatolia or Asia Minor, has been endowed with the homes of people and the locations of events in both the Old and the New Testaments. Only the land of Palestine has been linked more closely to the Bible than Anatolia. From the Tigris and Euphrates Rivers that flowed out of Eden to the churches of Revelation, from Adam and Eve to the Apostle John, biblical images, places, people, the words and their actions have conferred a unique legacy on Turkey. Here Abraham heard the call of God to worship Him alone; here Christians received their name; and from here Christianity spread into the Western world. The gifts and the responsibility of these visions are the heritage of Christians everywhere.

Biblical writers were intent to show that God worked through and was revealed in human history and in real places. The themes of God's inexorable justice and God's covenant with those who continue faithful to Him to bring about redemption pervade the Bible.

While some of the people of the Bible are probably legendary or even symbolic, many really lived. The events that they were a part of—the journeys, the battles, the visions—

happened in actual places known to the writers. Many of those places can be seen today; their major geographic identities, the rivers, mountains and shores, are relatively unchanged. Likewise, of the Old Testament references, the Anatolian places of Abraham's home of Harran, the land of Ararat, and the center of the Hittite Empire can be visited. Of the New Testament, some of the sophistication that distinguished the residents of 1st-century Antioch is on display through the mosaics in the Hatay Museum of Antakya; the ravages of time and the collapse of paganism show in the collapse of the beautiful Temple to Diana in Ephesus. John's message in the Book of Revelation has immortalized the seven churches he addressed in western Anatolia because of his portentous vision of the last days. With all of these, this country shares with Palestine the ancient identity of the Holy Land of the Bible.

The development of the monotheistic religions was concentrated in the Middle East. Judaism, Christianity, and Islam—the great religions of the Book, to use the Muslim phrase—originated here. This concentration is striking. What has there been about this land and its people that has inspired so much human vision of God? Certainly Christianity and Islam draw on the Judaic vision. Certainly the concentration of Judaic thought and practice in the Middle East influenced the development of the other two. Historians also point to the presence of oral accounts predating even the biblical records that contributed to the community ethos. And certainly the conditions of life, the challenges and the esthetic appreciation of the land have contributed to religious understanding.

Perhaps it is the physical search for religious truth yet to be revealed that has always attracted pilgrims. Probably it is in the discipline of the physical and spiritual search that each pilgrim finds his or her own visions and meanings.

Through the illustrations and text this book presents the people and places in Turkey to which there are biblical references. Current Turkish proper names are given in parentheses the first time the biblical names are used. The quotations are from *The Holy Bible, New Revised Standard Version* (Oxford University Press, 1989). Such quotations are identified in the text in italics. A reading list at the end offers suggestions for further study. The book is arranged chronologically, beginning with the poetry of Genesis and leading through the visions of Paul and John and their disciples. The author hopes that the visual images and the written words may convey some of the wonder and respect she has discovered for this Holy Land.

THE OLD TESTAMENT

Genesis: the Places and the People of Anatolia

The majestic poetry of Genesis begins with the images of creation, with darkness and a mighty wind out of which, day by day, God brought forth order and life and blessing. Even in English translations a dignity and awe resonate through the words.

> *And the Lord God planted a kingdom in Eden, in the*
> * east;*
> *and there he put the man whom he had formed.*
> *Out of the ground the Lord God made to grow*
> *every tree that is pleasant to the sight and good for*
> * food,*
> *the tree of life also in the midst of the garden,*
> *and the tree of the knowledge of good and evil.*
>
> (Gen. 2:8–9)

Archaeologists and historians looking for the origins and complexities of human development point to the few concentrations around the world of wild plants and animals that have become today's food sources. Of these locations, the Middle East, particularly the region called the Fertile Crescent, stands out because of the continuing role its residents have played in domesticating and distributing the improved stock. This concentration does not locate the kingdom; it does, however heighten the significance of Turkey as one of the homelands of very early humankind.

With the image of the tree of knowledge the writers of the Bible introduce the questions on which they are intent: How does God work in human life? Is the relationship between God and humankind static? With what do we come before God at the end? What sin, what sacrifice, what grace inform our relationship? We can trace the developing experience and understanding that we have gained as we work through history in the biblical references in Turkey, but the questions remain.

The Tigris and Euphrates Rivers

A river flows out of Eden to water the garden,
and from there it divides and becomes four branches.
The name of the first is Pishon;
it is the one that flows around the whole land of
    Havilah,
where there is gold;
and the gold of that land is good;
bdellium and onyx stone are there.
The name of the second river is Gihon;
it is the one that flows around the whole land of
    Cush.
The name of the third river is Tigris,
which flows east of Assyria.
And the fourth river is the Euphrates.

                              (Gen. 2:10–14)

Genesis presents the garden of Eden as a place of gold and precious stones, fruit trees, beautiful singing birds, a pleasant evening breeze, and finally including a partner helper for the man who has dominion over all—an idyllic paradise.

The geography of Eden is described only by the four streams that branch on leaving Eden. Two of them still carry their ancient names, the Tigris and the Euphrates, and both of them rise in the mountains of eastern Turkey. The basin between these two is known as that "between the rivers," or "Mesopotamia" (Gr. *mesos*—middle, and *potamos*—rapids); it is usually thought of as the land south of Turkey's border. After the thousands of seasons of harvesting its produce, farmers continue to find it fruitful. As for the rivers' resources, they are increasingly critical elements in the development and political stability of the region.

The headwaters of the Tigris converge in Lake Hazar in the valley between the Hazar and Mastar mountains northwest of Diyarbakir in southeastern Anatolia. From there the river flows about 300 km southeast gathering volume and strength, continuing through Iraq to the Persian Gulf. From Diyarbakir south the river was once open to shipping for commercial purposes; among the boats used were rafts floated on inflated skins. A series of dams on the river and its tributaries are part of the huge Southeast Anatolia Project (Güney Anadolu Projesi) that contributes to the hydroelectric power and irrigation of southeast Turkey, and that intensifies the potential conflicts between Turkey and its neighbors who also depend on the water.

The Euphrates is a longer and more complex river system than the Tigris. Two main streams, the northern Karasu and the southern Murat, rise in Turkey's northeast. Tributaries of the Karasu start in the snows of the mountains around Erzurum and then flow generally west for 350 km to the recently built Keban Dam near Elazığ. The southern Murat comes from multiple streams north of Ağrı; like the Karasu it also flows west about 400 km to empty into the same Keban Dam. Once joined, as the Euphrates the river continues southwest through the even larger Atatürk Dam and on another 450 km past the site of ancient Carchemish, where it crosses into Syria, emptying eventually into the Persian Gulf.

Was it for the writers of Genesis that these rivers brought so much richness to their lives that they believed they rose in Paradise? Or, with the image of the tree of life in Eden, did they marvel at the water that flowed without ceasing in the desert?

How much traffic they have carried! Flood-time and drought, war and peace, people with their commerce and their ideas, their skills and their pleasures, have enjoyed the use of these roads to speed their affairs. How much fertility!

Some of the early awakening in the history of human civilization took place on the slopes of the northern mountains of Mesopotamia. Here in what are now identified as Syria, Iraq and Turkey, people began cultivating wheat, olives and peas about 11,500 years ago. This activity marks the transition from nomadic hunting and gathering to intentional control of our environment. Called by some, "The Neolithic Revolution," this is a milestone in human development. From being at the mercy of the elements and the luck of the hunt, people changed to planting and harvesting the crops they chose. To do so, they had to stay put long enough to tend those crops; they had to find safe places to store their harvest. They had to cooperate with each other in order to harvest enough to see them through the winter until the next harvesting season. When the new life-style worked, the harvest satisfied everyone; it also produced extra so that specialized skills were needed and could be afforded, those of merchants and lawmakers, of artists and priests.

Adam and Eve

The Lord God took the man and put him in the garden of Eden to till it and keep it. And the Lord God commanded the man, "You may freely eat of every tree of the garden; but of the tree of the knowledge of good and evil you shall not eat, for in the day that you eat of it you shall die."

Then the Lord God said, "It is not good that the man should be alone; I will make him a helper as his partner." So out of the ground the Lord God formed every animal of the field and every bird of the air, and brought them to the man to see what he would call them; and whatever the man called every living creature, that was its name. The man gave names to all cattle, and to the birds of the air, and to every animal of the field; but for the man there was not found a helper as his partner. So the Lord God caused a deep sleep to fall upon the man, and he slept; then he took one of his ribs and closed up its place with flesh. And the rib that the Lord God had taken from the man he made into a woman and brought her to the man. Then the man said,

"This at last is bone of my bones
and flesh of my flesh;
this one shall be called Woman,
for out of Man this one was taken.". . .

Now the serpent was more crafty than any other wild animal that the Lord God had made. He said to the woman, "Did God say, 'You shall not eat from any tree in the garden'?" The woman said to the serpent, "We may eat of the fruit of the trees in the garden; but God said, 'You shall not eat of the fruit of the tree that is in the middle of the garden, nor shall you touch it, or you shall die.'" But the serpent said to the woman, "You will not die; for God knows that when you eat of it your eyes will be opened, and you will be like God, knowing good and evil."

(Gen. 2:15–23; 3:1–5)

The garden of Eden is an intangible, with all evidence so far pointing to the earliest Adams and Eves living in Africa, not in the Middle East. However, probably for the people relating the oral traditions, as it was for those later on who set them down in writing, the land between the Tigris and the Euphrates had been their ancestors' home as far back as anyone could remember. This was where the ancient heroes of the tribe had lived; this was what the mothers sang about in their lullabies.

The land between the rivers, Mesopotamia, is a fertile land; it has a haunting beauty. For varying reasons and from time immemorial, it has been so desirable that people have fought over it—Turkey's land included. Perhaps the insight of the human-divine interaction from the original conflict was memorialized in the first tragedy:

> *Now the man knew his wife Eve, and she conceived and bore Cain, saying, "I have produced a man with the help of the Lord." Next she bore his brother Abel. Now Abel was a keeper of sheep, and Cain a tiller of the ground. In the course of time Cain brought to the Lord an offering of the fruit of the ground, and Abel for his part brought of the firstlings of his flock, their fat portions. Now the Lord had regard for Abel and his offering, but for Cain and his offering he had no regard. So Cain was very angry, and his countenance fell. The Lord said to Cain, "Why are you angry, and why has your countenance fallen? If you do well, will you not be accepted? And if you do not do well, sin is lurking at the door; its desire is for you, but you must master it."*
>
> *Cain said to his brother Abel, "Let us go out to the field." And when they were in the field, Cain rose up against his brother Abel, and killed him. Then the Lord said to Cain, "Where is your brother Abel?" He said, "I do not know; am I my brother's keeper?" And the Lord said, "What have you done? Listen; your brother's blood is crying out to me from the ground!"*
>
> (Gen. 4:1-11)

The revolution did not happen smoothly; there were years of drought or flood or fire when the harvests were destroyed. One of its tragedies is dramatized in this story of shepherding and farming that do not combine well on the same land. Many times floods or drought or fire must have destroyed the crops and killed the livestock. Individuals wavered between investing in the new ways of agriculture and holding to the familiar rugged existence of hunting. Groups of people—both those who were brothers and those who were outsiders—competed, not always amicably, for what they considered good. Over, and over, and over again.

Noah and His Sons' Sons' Sons

Noah

The Lord saw that the wickedness of humankind was great in the earth, and that every inclination of the thoughts of their hearts was only evil continually. And the Lord was sorry that he had made humankind on the earth, and it grieved him to his heart. So the Lord said, "I will blot out from the earth the human beings I have created—people together with animals and creeping things and birds of the air, for I am sorry that I have made them." But Noah found favor in the sight of the Lord.

. . . Now the earth was corrupt in God's sight, and the earth was filled with violence. . . . God said to Noah, "I have determined to make an end of all flesh, . . . Make yourself an ark of cypress wood; make rooms in the ark, and cover it inside and out with pitch. . . ."

. . . And Noah with his sons and his wife and his sons'
wives went into the ark to escape the waters of the
flood. Of clean animals, and of animals that are not
clean, and of birds, and of everything that creeps on the
ground, two and two, male and female, went into the
ark with Noah, as God had commanded Noah. And
after seven days the waters of the flood came on the
earth. . . .

And the waters swelled on the earth for one hundred
fifty days.   (Gen. 6:5–14, 7:7–24 passim)

Recently discovered geologic evidence in the Mediterranean,
Aegean, and Black Sea regions, coupled with similarities in
many Flood stories, have led scholars to suggest that the
legend originated in at least one actual, sudden, catastrophic event. The relatively smaller fresh water inland lake
of today's Black Sea was inundated about 12,000 years ago
by a salt sea that crashed across the land barrier now split
by the Bosphorus Straits. People living on its shores had
barely days to save themselves and their moveable property
by scrambling for the high ground of the mountains. What
caused the event is still being debated: A volcanic eruption,
an abrupt warming of the earth's atmosphere, a huge earth-
quake? Or all of the above?

Perhaps the stories preserve the responses in which the
bewildered survivors found comfort in the face of their
questions of why such devastation overwhelmed them, and
why they—alone among a multitude—survived.

The Flood stories include those of the *Eridu Genesis*, the *Myth of Atrahasis*, and the *Gilgamesh Epic*, all using the crisis of a major flood. Most of the *Gilgamesh Epic* was taken up with Gilgamesh's adventures and his search for perpetual youth. One adventure involved his mentor, Utnapistim, whose story parallels Noah's: Because he knew that the rains were coming, he built a ship and took into it all varieties of animals. After many days Utnapistim sent a dove out to learn if the waters had receded. On landing he gave thanks to the supreme goddess Ishtar who wore a many-colored necklace. In the *Myth of Atrahasis*, the hero was warned by the gods to build a boat to save his family and his animals. Reminiscent of the rainbow, a necklace of blue stones distinguished the Mother Goddess. The *Eridu Genesis*, a similar tale, probably centered in the flood plain of the Tigris and Euphrates Rivers.

Each account concerns the issue of how God works in human life. The Gilgamesh Epic recognized human transience: Gilgamesh was unable to find eternal life. The Bible recognized human frailty: Noah got drunk on his first grape harvest. With varying levels of insight, the concept of mutual responsibility—God's covenant with humankind in the visual symbol of the rainbow—underlay the lessons of Utnapishtim, Atrahasis and Noah.

The Sons' Sons' Sons

In attempting to give form and meaning to the relationships between Israel and her neighbors, the narrator-writers of Genesis constructed a genealogy that began with Noah and his three sons (Gen. 10:1–32). Probably it was as accurate and thoroughly researched a listing as was possible for its time. The writers apparently knew more about the people who lived near them than those at a distance. That is, for instance, the children of Ashur and Aram with whom they had frequent contact were more detailed than those of Riphath and Togarmah who are thought to have lived a thousand kilometers to the north.

Not all of Noah's descendents can be traced today, nor do all the peoples on earth fit neatly into this "Table of Nations." Some of the names are confusing: Is there a difference between the Hamitic Ludim and the Semitic Lud? Or are these two families who intermarried? Next, Heth is thought to refer to the Hittites of central Anatolia. But Heth is named as one of Ham's descendents, and Ham's family should be concentrated in North Africa. Could not these discrepancies suggest that people moved around in biblical times as they do today, and that not only the writers but the people themselves may have gotten mixed up?

Genealogy

The Bible is an inspired account of the understandings we have gotten over time of our relations with God. This is primary. In addition, as biblical archaeology has developed, the Bible has served for the researchers as one of the earliest records of human history. Archaeology has often broadened our understanding of biblical events, in the present instance as a reference for identifying many groups of ancient Middle Eastern peoples and their locations.

If we accept the confusions and uncertainties, the genealogy given in Genesis makes a useful outline for the interconnections among the peoples, in addition to outlining their family relationships.

Of Noah's presumed descendents who appear in later Old Testament references and who had connections with Anatolia, these are particularly interesting:

Anatolia seems to have been the home of most of the Japhethites:

Gomer, Magog, Madai, Javan, Tubal, Meshech

Gomer's Family: Ashkenaz, Riphath, Togarmah

Javan's Family: Tarshish

Ham's family members are the Hamites. His family members in Anatolia included:

Mizraim, Canaan, Cush

Mizraim's Family: Lydians, Caphtorites (the Philistines)

Canaan's Family: Heth, the Hivites

Cush's Family: Nimrod

Shem's family members are the Semites. His family members in Anatolia included:

Asshur, Arpachshad, Lud, Aram

Arpachshad's Family: Eber, Terah, Abram, Nahor, Haran

The words "Semites" and "Semitic" to define a person or a language are still current usage, and "Hamite" and "Hamitic" occur occasionally. But "Japhethite" and

"Japhetic," which the dictionary says used to mean "Indo-European," are almost non-existent.

The Japhethites: Gomer

Gomer's family members—Ashkenaz, Riphath, Togarmah—apparently were concentrated in northeast Asia Minor, in southern Russia, and eastward to the Caspian Sea. One identification links Gomer with the Cimmerians who migrated to Turkey in the 8th century BCE after being driven out of Russia by the Scythians. They invaded Urartu (the area of eastern Turkey around Lake Van) in about 714 BCE; sixty years later they had moved farther west to take and hold Sardis briefly.

Ashkenaz is the supposed ancestor of the Armenians. The early history of the Armenians appears in the 6th-century BCE records of the kings of Urartu when the Armenians invaded the kings' territory.

Riphath's identity has not yet been established. Togarmah has variously been identified with the city of Gurun in south central Turkey, or, in the similar name "Thargamos," as the ancestor of the Georgians. If they are the Georgians, they are represented in northeastern Turkey in the remains of the stately churches built during the reign of the Bagratid rulers, particularly King Bagrat III (r. 980–1014 CE), King David II (r. 1089–1125), and Queen Tamara (r. 1184–1213). (The Bagratids themselves claimed descent from King David and from Herod the Great.)

The Medes

The Medes (Madai), associated with the Persians for their unalterable law (Dan. 6:8), seem to have started as a named group in the Caucasus like other members of Japheth's family, and to have moved into eastern Turkey and northern Iran in the 9th or 8th century BCE.

Cyaxarses, the Median king from 625 to 585 BCE, brought an end to the Assyrian Empire when he took Nineveh in 612 and sacked Harran in 610. Not long thereafter, in 550, the Medes themselves became subjects of the Persians under Cyrus the Great. They then cooperated with him to help capture Sardis in 546.

Javan

Javan, the fourth of Japheth's sons, was the name given to the region of the northwestern coastal areas of Anatolia and northeastern Greece. The word survives in the name of the region, "Ionia," and in "Yunanistan," the Turkish word for "Greece."

Neither Ionia nor Greece is clearly identified in the Old Testament, but there seems to be a glancing reference to Greek history in the vision of Daniel in Chapter 11. This vision involves the Persian king in whose court Daniel spent his last years and who may have been patterned on Cyrus the Great (6th century BCE; note Isa. 45:1-3). Cyrus captured Sardis from Croesus and authorized that the temple be rebuilt in Jerusalem. The warrior king who surpasses all others in Daniel's vision is thought possibly to be Alexander the Great. The division of his kingdom could refer to the careers of his generals who took his place at his death: Seleucis, Antigonus, and Lysimachus. It is these references that suggest the date of Daniel to be around 150 BCE when those men's careers would have been known:

> *Three more kings will appear in Persia, and the fourth will far surpass all the others in wealth; and when he has extended his power through his wealth, he will rouse the whole world against the kingdom of Greece. Then there will appear a warrior king. He will rule a vast kingdom and will do what he chooses. But as soon as he is established, his kingdom will be shattered and split up north, south, east and west. It will not pass to any descendants, nor will any of his successors have an empire like his. . . . (Dan. 11:2-4)*

Tubal and Meshech

Tubal and Meshech are commonly named together in the Old Testament; they are therefore assumed to have been political (and maybe military) allies. Their homeland was the mountainous region of central Anatolia, a place rich in copper and tin ores. An 8th century BCE Meshech king, Midas, was one of the many enemies of the Assyrian king Sargon II. (Sargon appears in several biblical references, such as 2 Kings 17 and Isaiah 14:3-21.) Items from Midas' presumed tomb in Gordium are displayed in the Museum of Anatolian Civilizations in Ankara.

By the time of the Prophet Ezekiel (6th century BCE), the people of Tubal, Meshech, and Javan were known to the biblical writers as slave traders and metallurgists. Their skill in forging swords had become almost proverbial; their reputation as swordsmen unmanned their enemies. Thus, intending to give hope to the Jewish exiles in Babylon, Ezekiel prophesied their downfall:

> *There are Meshech and Tubal with all their hordes, with their burial around them, all of them strengthless and slain by the sword, men who once struck terror into the land of the living.* (Ezek. 32:26)

Among the people resident in Central Anatolia in the 8th century BCE, the Phrygians might be related to Meshech. The connection could be purely adventitious, but Greek historians name the Phrygian kings Midas, a name that echoes in records of Meshech, but that does not establish the family connection. Another possible connection appears in designs and shapes on metal cauldrons that were found in Phrygian graves. These designs indicate that they had commerce with Urartu to the east. More importantly, these cauldrons may show a commerce in goods and ideas among the Eastern artisans of the Van region, those of Greece, and those of the Western Etruscans of Italy.

Perhaps the Phrygians came from the Balkans; perhaps they intermarried with the Hittites who were still living in Central Anatolia after the invasions of the Sea Peoples. Their origins are uncertain, but they are the first group to be identified in western Anatolia after the disappearance of the Hittites in the 11th century BCE.

The remains of a Phrygian foundry have been identified in Midas Şehri south of Eskişehir where there was an 8th-century BCE temple to the Asiatic goddess of fertility, Cybele. The priestess of Cybele was expected to preside over and bless the dangerous casting of the metal items such as swords and images. That ceremony was intended to insure the safety of the metal workers and to add the frighteningly supernatural strength and trustworthiness to weapons of the hordes from Meshech and Tubal.

The Hamites: Mizraim

Ham's Anatolian families are thought to trace their ancestry to his sons Mizraim, Canaan, and Cush. Mizraim has connections with western Turkey, Canaan with central Turkey, and Cush with southeastern Turkey.

Mizraim, one of Ham's sons, is thought by some to be the forefather of the Lydians. In classical Western history, accounts of the Lydians begin in the 9th century BCE. Their small territory lay inland from the Aegean, but, even without a seaport, they had become a force to reckon with by the 6th century BCE, in no small part because of their contribution to world trade. They are credited with being the first to establish a guaranteed standard value in their coinage. Their last independent king, Croesus (560–546), was defeated by the Persian Cyrus the Great when he took the capital Sardis. Both the persons and the history of Lydia come alive in the account of the 5th-century BCE Greek historian Herodotus of Halicarnassus (Bodrum).

With the reputation that Sardis had in business dealings, it would seem reasonable to expect that some Jewish traders were living in Sardis as expatriates long before the 6th century BCE. Such resident communities were apparently common in the commercial centers throughout the Middle East. An Old Testament reference in connection with the Lydians and Sardis as a far-away place occurs in the short book of the Prophet Obadiah, written perhaps in the 6th century. Obadiah (v. 20) speaks of the hope for the return "*of the exiles of Jerusalem who are in Sepharad.*" Sepharad and Sardis are the same in this quotation. These exiles may have been among the many Jews whom Nebuchanezzar's officer Nebuzaradan dispersed from Jerusalem when he destroyed the city and the temple in 586 BCE (2 Kings 25:11).

Caphtorites: Sea Peoples

The Caphtorites, children of Ham's son Mizraim like the Lydians, have various identifications that suggest that they may have been some of the many tribes from the Balkans, Thrace, or Crete who swept across the eastern Mediterranean in the 13th and 12th centuries BCE.

The Egyptian pharaoh Ramses III defeated one of the more organized of these migratory groups in the early 12th century. He then settled them as neighbors to Israel on the southeast coast of the Mediterranean. It is through his accounts that they came to be known as the Sea Peoples, and later as the Philistines.

The Sea Peoples caused havoc all along the eastern Mediterranean. The destruction of Homer's Troy and the downfall of the Hittite Empire are attributed to them. Ramses III reported that they also destroyed Carchemish (one of its many disasters). The account of the Assyrian king Tiglath-Pileser I reports his fight on the upper Tigris against one of these tribes whom he calls the Mushki. He and they were contesting the control of iron-rich Anatolia at the time that iron was more valuable than gold.

The devastation that the Sea Peoples brought was so great that it took at least two hundred years for those few who survived to recover. The ravage was not only a physical destruction but also one of traditions and culture. The Hittites' written records stop about 1180 BCE, thought to be when the less literary invaders overcame them.

Another recently proposed theory is that this migration may have coincided with a period of many and frequent devastating earthquakes in the eastern Mediterranean. With those natural disasters would have come a periodic and sometimes profound disruption of life.

Canaan: the Hittites

Ham's son Canaan is the presumed progenitor of the Hittites (Heth); thus they would be cousins of the Sea Peoples. Not long ago the Hittites were known only as a name in the Old Testament whose importance could be dismissed along with Rebecca's complaint about Esau's wives: "*I am weary to death of Hittite women!*" (Gen. 27:46)

Then in 1906 explorers began identifying hieroglyphs and sculptures that fit with Egyptian and Assyrian references to the people of Kheta and the land of the Hatti, rivals of the Egyptians. Next, thousands of cuneiform tablets were found in the archives of a royal city in central Turkey. A copy of the treaty between the Hittites and the Egyptians, drawn up after the Battle of Kadesh (1285 BCE), was also found in the same cache. This is now considered to be the first known treaty signed by equal sovereign powers. Although the treaty appeared on pylons in Luxor, the Hittite role in the battle had been discounted by historians because of the Egyptian attitude towards them. (The Egyptians were a known power; the Hittites were only a minor reference in the Bible.) The translation of the inscriptions and the acceptance of Hittite importance was further speeded by the bilingual Hittite-Phoenician inscription discovered at Karatepe in southwestern Turkey in 1946. With these and additional written records, archaeologists are still broadening their understanding of the power and the extent of the Hittite Empire that controlled much of central Anatolia for about a thousand years in the 2nd millennium BCE.

The main center of the empire (but not the capital) was Hatussas (Boğazkale) east of Ankara. The height of the Old Hittite Empire came during the reign of Mursilis 1 whose power stretched from central Turkey into Syria. He conquered Babylon in 1594 BCE. After a period of Hittite decline, Suppiluliumas 1 (1380–1346 BCE) led the New Hittites even farther into Syria. His son fought the Egyptians; the outcome of that battle led to the Treaty of Kadesh. Following the disasters caused by the invasions of the Sea Peoples in the 12th century BCE that marked the end of the Hittite Empire, smaller Neo-Hittite principalities in southeastern Turkey (Malatya, Carchemish, Karatepe) flourished for another four hundred years.

The Hittites also had properties—though perhaps held only by private individuals—as far south as Canaan: The Hittites owned the land in Hebron that Abraham bought in order to have a place to bury his wife Sarah. The Bible records him as the alien and the Hittites as *the people of the land.* (Gen. 25:7) After bargaining, Abraham acquired the best grave-site they had at Machpelah, a field with a cave just east of Hebron. There he also was buried (Gen. 23, 25:9–10). Other scattered biblical references to the Hittites include that of Uriah for whose wife, Bathsheba, king David lusted (2 Samuel 11), and to the chariots and horses that her son Solomon imported from the Hittite kings (1 Kings 10:29).

Cush

Cush, Ham's third son with Anatolian connections, is generally identified with Ethiopia. However, one man of his family stands out as a place name in Anatolia and as a major king.

Cush was the father of Nimrod, who began to show
himself a man of might on earth; and he was a mighty
hunter before the Lord. . . . . His kingdom in the begin-
ning consisted of Babel, Erech, and Accad, all of them
in the land of Shinar. From that land he migrated to
Asshur and built Nineveh, Rehoboth-Ir, Calah, and
Resen, a great city between Nineveh and Calah. (Gen.
10:7-12)

The families of Cush and Shem's son Asshur must have met
and mingled frequently since both are associated with
southeastern Anatolia. Nimrod appears as a geographic
name several places. Two Anatolian mountains carry it; both
are volcanic, one north of Lake Van, a second northeast of
Adıyaman. The first Nemrut Dağı is probably only tem-
porarily quiescent: Hot water and active sulfur vents in the
caldera are a vivid reminder of its true nature. A lava flow
from this mountain dammed the river that emptied Lake
Van thousands of years ago; that blockage made Van both
the largest lake in Turkey and the world's largest soda lake.

Antiochus I of Commagene (c. 62-38 BCE) memorialized
himself on the second Nemrut Dağı where temples for him
faced the rising and the setting sun. Enormous statues of
Persian/Greek gods are lined above the altars, their bodies
still in place but their heads toppled into the rubble below.

Perhaps both of these mountains were named for the son of
Cush who in the Bible was the mighty hunter, the man of
might, the first great king.

The Semites

Shem's family connections in Anatolia are through Asshur, Lud, Aram, and Arpachshad. Lud may be the same people as the Lydians who may also have been related to Ham; otherwise their place in Anatolia is dubious. The others are known through both biblical and historical records.

Asshur, Aram, and Arpachshad are probably eponymous ancestors of groups located generally north or northeast of Israel. How far into Anatolia and at what times their influence extended are questions still debated. These three families had a common tie because they all spoke a Semitic language. (This was not true of all of Shem's descendants).

Asshur

Asshur is the presumed father of the Assyrians. Asshur (also Assur) was both the name of the oldest capital of Assyria (located on the Tigris River south of Mosul) and of the main pagan god. The records of Assyria go back five thousand years; the Assyrian Empire, one of the major political forces in history, lasted from about 1500 to 600 BCE, roughly the same time as the more western Hittite Empire. At its greatest extent it took in most of what today is called the Middle East, with its center in the northern basin of the Tigris River.

Of the kings of the Assyrian Empire who affected events in Anatolia, the following stand out because of their battles with neighbors, including Israel.

Tiglath-Pileser I (fl. 1120 BCE) defeated the Mushki in eastern Anatolia. He went on to dominate most of the groups, including the Hurrians, from Lake Van to Cappadocia, forcing them to pay him tribute. Among his records, the laws relating to marriage, property rights and creditors have helped date other rulers and events.

Tiglath-Pileser III (r. 745–727 BCE) was known in the Old Testament as Pul. In the time of Azariah, Tiglath-Pileser III invaded Judea (2 Kings 15:17–20). He also fought the Urartians around Lake Van.

Sargon II (r. 722–705 BCE), the son of Tiglath-Pileser III, finished the conquest of the Urartians started by his father. One of his enemies was King Midas of Gordium. Sargon lost his life either fighting in Tabal (perhaps the region of Cilicia—Turkish Çukurova) or in a coup in his palace in Assur.

Sennacherib (r. 705–681 BCE) took over after the murder of his father, Sargon II. When the residents of Tarsus revolted against Assyrian rule in 696 BCE, King Sennacherib destroyed their city. He went on to besiege Jerusalem during the reign of King Hezekiah and to send the Israelites into exile. Sennacherib was later murdered by two of his sons who fled to Urartu (Ararat) for safety: "*As he was worshiping in the house of his god Nisroch, his sons Adrammelech and Sharezer killed him with the sword, and they escaped into the land of Ararat.*" (2 Kings 19:37).

Aram

Aram, the last named of Shem's sons, is the presumed ancestor of the Aramaeans. Today's Syrians are thought to be among his descendants. In the Old Testament Abraham's nephew Bethuel, the son of Nahor, and his daughter Rebecca who married Isaac, were Aramaeans from Paddan-aram. The symbolic power of this identity is evident in the charge that Moses gave the Children of Israel: He told them that when they entered the Promised Land they were to take the first fruits of their produce, give them to the priest as an offering, and recite, "*A wandering Aramean was my ancestor; he went down into Egypt and lived there as an alien. . .*" (Deut. 26:5)

The political weight of the Aramaeans is known from the many Middle Eastern nations with whom they fought, including the Hittites, the Assyrians, and the Israelites. The earliest non-biblical record of them comes from early-11th-century BCE inscriptions of the Assyrian king Tiglath-Pileser I.

Although the Assyrian Tiglath-Pileser III ended Aramaean independence in 732 BCE, their cultural importance increased afterwards. By the 7th century BCE all of Syria and most of Mesopotamia used the Semitic Aramaic language and alphabet. That language dominated the Middle East until the Hellenistic influence took over following Alexander the Great's conquest. It was one of the languages in which parts of Ezra, Daniel, and Jeremiah were written; one of its dialects was probably the language that Jesus spoke. Its alphabet is the basis of Hebrew, Arabic, and Syriac, and it later influenced the Armenian and Georgian alphabets. It remains the language today of the Syrian Orthodox Church whose ancient center in southeastern Turkey (part of old Assyria) is in the region of Tur Abdin ("the Plateau of the Servants of God") around the city of Mardin.

Chaldeans

The sovereignties of Assyria, Aramaea, and Chaldea over-lapped in geography and in time; their peoples share family identities. Assyria (2nd to mid-1st millennium BCE) encompassed much of eastern Turkey and Iraq, and also extended south into Egypt. Aramaea (1st millennium) perhaps was more limited, being concentrated north of Damascus. Chaldea (1st millennium) was centered near the head of the Persian Gulf. However, the Chaldeans were loosely organized Semitic tribal groups found throughout Mesopotamia and as far north as eastern Anatolia.

Chaldean astrologer/astronomer/magicians—Magi—studied the heavens and recorded what they saw for the purposes of worship and of understanding what was happening on earth. The names of the stars and the movements of the moon and the planets that they recorded underlie the math-ematics and astronomy we study today. Syrian Orthodox Christians celebrate a tradition at Christmas that their Wise Men—the Magi from the east—who saw the wondrous star at the birth of Jesus traveled through Tur Abdin on their way to Bethlehem.

In history Chaldeans played a critical role in battles between Assyria, Egypt, Babylon and Judah. Their military prowess was recorded on orthostats, depicting charioted warriors riding over their slain enemies, that lined the kings' processional way in Carchemish.

One of the tangles of history involved the Egyptian, Judean, and Chaldean armies. This began when the Egyptian pharaoh Necho and the Judean king Josiah fought each other at Carchemish, a ford and a marketplace on the Euphrates River. The encounter changed the history of the kingdom of Judah. At the time—the late 7th century BCE—Egypt and Assyria were allies. Thus, when Chaldean Babylon attacked Assyrian Nineveh in 621 BCE, Necho responded to Assyria's call for help. Necho landed his army on the Mediterranean coast north of Judah, miscalculating the political ambitions of Judah's strong king Josiah. Josiah had been carrying on a program of national revival in Jerusalem; he wanted, perhaps as the culmination of his reign, either to unite Judah and Israel to the north or to protect Babylon. Therefore he took Necho's appearance as a chance to strengthen his hand. Meeting at Carchemish, Necho tried to placate Josiah, saying that he had no quarrel with Judah. However, Josiah was bent on a fight, and so their armies became engaged at Meggido. Josiah was mortally wounded in the battle, and Judah's next kings were too weak to maintain an independent state. (II Chron. 35:20–25) For the writer of Revelation much later, Meqqido (or Armaqeddon) became the metaphor for the place of the final decisive battle between good and evil.

Pharaoh Necho went on to fight and defeat Babylon in 606; the next year he attacked the Chaldeans again, in Carchemish. But the Chaldeans were led by a vigorous, young prince Nebuchadnezzar who beat Necho soundly, forcing the exhausted Egyptians to withdraw from Syria and Palestine.

Not stopping there, Nebuchadnezzar followed up his victory in Carchemish by capturing Jerusalem in 597 and deporting its king Jehoiachim to Babylon. This is considered the beginning of the Babylonian exile for Israel. Historians speculate that if Josiah had not fought Necho in the first place, the Egyptians might have been strong enough to defeat Nebuchadnezzar and prevent his attack on Jerusalem.

Urartians

A second family of Aramaeans who were a political force in eastern Anatolia were the Urartians. Appearing early in the 13th century BCE, they called their country Bianili, and their capital Tushpa (near Van). At one time the Urartian holdings bordered Phrygia on the west; to the east their network of small fortress cities stretched as far as Lake Urmia in today's Iran.

The land of Urartu has two bearings on the biblical connections with eastern Anatolia. One is that the Urartians were known as vintners, as was Noah, who by legend was the first man to grow grapes. Another is as the location of the mountain in Ararat on which the legendary Noah's ark landed. The original form of the word for the land (the root three letters "rrt") can be translated both Ararat and Urartu. Mt. Ararat, the place that continues the use of the word, is the tallest mountain in Turkey (5123 m), but it is only one of many mountains in the original land of Urartu/Ararat. In the Koran, Noah's landing was on Mt. El-Judi (Cudi Dağı) which is also in Urartu not far from the Turkish-Iraqi border.

The political history of Urartu includes the names of the Assyrian Tiglath-Pileser III who defeated the Urartian Sarduri II in 743 BCE and Sargon II who completed the Urartian demise. Records of an Urartian chief minister in the 8th century speak of the diplomatic contacts he had with Egypt, Babylon, Mysia, Phrygia, and Syria. He said he knew twelve languages and could use four different writing systems. While this may have been self-aggrandizement, it points to Urartu's extensive international trade.

Arpachshad

Arpachshad was Shem's son, born two years after the Flood (Gen. 11:10). His family traditionally is thought to have been located at first in Mesopotamia, more specifically in Babylonia, although the family probably spread out over a large area. The members included Eber and his descendents, Terah, Nahor, and Haran who figure in southeastern Anatolia. Haran and Nahor were Terah's sons, as was Abram, the oldest son and the one to become *"the ancestor of a multitude of nations"* (Gen. 17:4).

Abraham and His Family in Anatolia

Abraham

The identities of Noah and his three sons as historic individuals are doubtful. These sons are usually considered eponymous ancestors, the real names or attributes of legendary leaders from which the groups reputedly derived their own names. The identity of Abraham (Abram at first) is a degree less problematic, though still a puzzle for scholars. Was he only a legend, the ideal patriarch? Or did this man really live? If so, when? Some time during the Bronze Age? Archaeologists can find evidence in contemporary records that might support several different dates any time between 5000 and 1200 BCE. Whether he was real or legend, why is he still important?

> *When Terah had lived seventy years, he became the father of Abram, Nahor, and Haran.*
>
> *Now these are the descendents of Terah. Terah was the father of Abram, Nahor, and Haran; and Haran was the father of Lot. Haran died before his father Terah in the land of his birth, in Ur of the Chaldeans. Abram and Nahor took wives; the name of Abram's wife was Sarai, and the name of Nahor's wife was Milcah. She was the daughter of Haran the father of Milcah and Iscah. Now Sarai was barren; she had no child.*

*Terah took his son Abram and his grandson Lot son of
Haran, and his daughter-in-law Sarai, his son Abram's
wife, and they went out together from Ur of the
Chaldeans to go into the land of Canaan; but when they
came to Haran, they settled there. The days of Terah
were two hundred five years; and Terah died in Haran.*

*Now the Lord said to Abram, "Go from your country
and your kindred and your father's house to the land
that I will show you. I will make of you a great nation,
and I will bless you, and make your name great, so that
you will be a blessing. I will bless those who bless you,
and the one who curses you I will curse; and in you all
the families of the earth shall be blessed.*

*So Abram went, as the Lord had told him; and Lot went
with him.* (Gen. 11:26–32; 12:1–4)

The classic interpretation of this account is of the coura-
geous reformer willing to risk breaking with his
community's traditions of polytheism to move his family to
a new land where he will establish the worship of One God.
He becomes the Patriarch, the head of the family whom God
blesses because he is faithful to God's commands. Thus this
is a parable of the covenant between God and humankind.
Some years later God rewards Abram's faithfulness with the
promise again that his descendents will be many, and in
token of that renames him "Abraham" or "*Exalted
Ancestor, Father of a Multitude.*" (Gen. 17)

As great a patriarch as he was, parts of the account are more
examples of the social customs of the time than examples

for today's living. For instance, there is Abraham's deception of Pharoah (Gen. 12:10-20) concerning his true relation to his wife Sarai in order to save his life. But whether or not Abraham was an historical person, a legendary symbol, or a bit of both, the figure in the Old Testament is of a remarkable leader.

Other puzzles associated with Abraham are the location of Ur, and the relation between Ur of the Chaldeans and Haran (Harran or Altınbaşak in Turkish). With the exploration of Tell al-Muqayyar in the 19th century, continued by Leonard Woolley after World War 1, the royal city of Ur has been generally accepted as this site in today's southern Iraq on the Euphrates flood plain. This southern Ur has many points in its favor. It is in Babylonia, and has provided a rich source of archaeological treasures and information about religious practices, royal life, and ordinary people's doings from about 5500 to 600 BCE. An even more telling coincidence is that the Chaldean Empire refers generally to southern Mesopotamia. Ur should be here.

But why, if Terah was intending to go to Canaan, did he wander all the way north to Harran? Did the easiest road there lead him 1200 km upstream—admittedly on a well-traveled trade route—for him then to turn back south 650 km across the Syrian Desert? It's not an impossible journey, and there is no evidence that he was compelled to take the shortest route.

On the other hand, archaeologists more recently have been discussing the idea that the land of the Chaldeans extended into what is now southeastern Turkey. This opens up the possibility that the reference is to a different Ur, namely Urfa. Urfa, or Şanlıurfa today, is about 50 km north of Harran. It, too, is an ancient city, a thriving city, a royal city. The main God worshipped in Urfa four thousand years ago was the same moon-god Sin that was worshipped in southern Chaldea. This god Sin was surrounded by a host of lesser gods, enough that if Abraham had transferred his allegiance to the One God it would have been a revolutionary decision.

There are even more difficult problems of identification. This Ur, or Urfa, is a living city, not a dead archaeological dig, and thus has never been excavated to determine its early importance. Moreover, northern Mesopotamia was only a Chaldean hinterland. Its early treasures—surely there are many—have not been uncovered and examined.

Perhaps an equally puzzling question is why so much is made of Terah having left Urfa to get only as far as Harran.

Urfa has an intriguing connection with Nimrod ("*the first on earth to become a mighty warrior. . . a mighty hunter before the Lord*" Gen. 10:8–9) and Abraham in Muslim legend. The local story goes that Abraham was born in one of the caves of Urfa and as a young man contested here with its King Nimrod over the issue of monotheism. Incensed by Abraham's determination to worship only God, Nimrod tried to kill him by throwing him off the citadel hill. But the One God protected Abraham by creating pools of water where he landed. The carp in those pools are considered so sacred that people will not catch them for food.

Whatever the location that is accepted for Ur, the identity of Harran is known both from local wisdom and from reference to it in Hurrian archives found in Nuzi (near Kerkuk in Iraq). Harran was a political and a religious center for the Hurrians in the 2nd millennium BCE. The king could have had one of his palaces here; it was an important center because its large temple to Sin attracted pilgrims for centuries. Along with that worship, Harran was an educational center that continued far into the Christian era. The Assyrian priests of the moon-god studied the heavens as astrologer/astronomers. The ruins of a 7th-or 8th-century CE Omayyad great mosque and university walled complex lie to the north of the main buildings of Harran. A high tower or minaret looms over that complex; perhaps the shadow of this *gnomon* was used by the Assyrians to measure the sun and the moon and the stars in their courses.

Terah, Abraham, and their families remained in Harran for an indefinite time, at least long enough for Abraham to develop some lasting identity with the place. These ties lasted through his grandson's family. Today's residents are proud of their associations with Abraham: They cherish a gentle, grassy slope as his traditional home and the place where they say he heard God's call. Along with that, they water their sheep outside the city walls at a well they know as "B'ir Yakup" (Jacob's Well).

Isaac and Rebecca

Harran continued to be thought of as Abraham's home country for several generations after he had settled in Canaan. When Abraham realized that it was time to find a wife for his son Isaac, he commissioned his servant to return to Harran. He did not want Isaac marrying one of the Canaanite women who worshipped Baal. Rather, he told his head servant, *Put your hand under my thigh and I will make you swear by the Lord, the God of heaven and earth, that you will not get a wife for my son from the daughters of the Canaanites, among whom I live, but will go to my country and to my kindred and get a wife for my son Isaac.* (Gen. 24:3–4)

The list of items of the bride price that the servant took is some evidence of Abraham's prosperity, of his approval of Isaac, and of the level of what was expected in order to cement a marriage contract in Harran. In addition to the gold and silver and costly garments such as were usually given to royalty, the servant took ten camels, perhaps the most valuable of all the presents. Not only were camels tokens of wealth, they may not have been known in the region of Harran much before the 12th century BCE. This date therefore might help establish the date when Abraham lived.

Arriving in Harran, the servant went to the village well where he expected to find the women drawing water in the evening. In answer to his prayer, he met Rebecca who matched the description of the girl for whom he was searching. Rebecca was the daughter of Abraham's nephew Bethuel. Upon her consent and that of her parents and her brother Laban, the bride price was accepted and she accompanied the servant back to Canaan to marry Isaac.

When Abraham died, Isaac and his half-brother Ishmael (son of the slave girl Hagar) buried him with his wife Sarah in the cave of Machpelah in Hebron, the property that Abraham had bought from Ephron the Hittite years before. (Gen. 24, 25:8–10) (Abraham's wife's name, like his, had been changed by then from Sarai to Sarah.)

Jacob and Rachel

The story of Jacob parallels Isaac's in that he turned again to the land of his mother and grandfather to solve his family problem. However, this time it was not the servant, but rather the prospective bridegroom who made the journey to Harran, *"the land of the people of the east."* (Gen. 29:1) This time, also, it was not as a princely suitor that he presented himself; rather he was a fugitive escaping from his brother Esau's fury. Jacob had cheated Esau out of his birthright and his father's blessing.

Except for the new generation living there, very little had changed over the years. Much of the social life apparently still revolved around the village well, for it was there that the shepherds gathered to water their flocks. A huge stone protected the water of the well from accidental pollution. The custom was for the shepherds to wait for everyone to gather before the stone was removed.

When Jacob was told that the shepherdess approaching was Laban's daughter, Jacob jumped to help her and rolled the stone away for her to water her father's sheep. Then he kissed her, weeping probably only partly in relief that he had found his kinsfolk.

Having explained that he was a close relative, he was welcomed by Laban who engaged him to work. The agreement as Jacob understood it was that his pay for seven years of labor would be Laban's daughter in marriage. Seven years might have equaled the riches that had been his mother Rebecca's bride price. At the end of that time, Jacob discovered that the daughter Laban had given him was the older Leah of the lovely eyes, not the younger Rachel whom he loved. So he contracted for a second seven years of labor. (This was only one of many of the relations between Jacob and his family that were dishonest and manipulative. Gen. 48, 49)

During the years that Jacob lived in Harran, eleven of his twelve sons were born, those whose names became the names of the Twelve Tribes of Israel. Only Benjamin, whose mother Rachel died in his birth, was not born in Harran.

It is easy to imagine that present-day Harran is much as it might have been for Abraham and Jacob. Except for the 11th/12th-century Crusader fortress and the Great Mosque, the countryside in the first years of the 21st century seems much the same farm and pasture land. One sees shepherds following sheep, children playing near their homes, the seasons steadily coming and going. The real scene tempts one also to see the men as historic persons pasturing their flocks here in the not-too-distant past, capably coping with day-to-day problems.

Genesis only hints that Abraham's life might not have been easy, that his acceptance of God's call might have brought down the wrath of his tribe on his head. That possibly poignant conflict when he defies his community's long-entrenched beliefs is caught in the short phrase, "*the one who curses you I will curse.*" The parallel follows Jacob when he takes Esau's place before Isaac: "*Cursed be everyone who curses you, and blessed be everyone who blesses you.*" (Gen. 27:29)

Whether Abraham is the historic patriarch, and Jacob (later Israel) is the father of nations, or whether they are symbols of many visionaries, in spite of their flaws, in the fire of their visions our own faith in One God is kindled.

THE NEW TESTAMENT

The Dispersed Followers

Anatolia figures more in the New Testament than in the Old Testament. In both, decisive events for Judaism and Christianity occurred in Anatolia, but, naturally, those in the New Testament are more recent than those in the Old. In both, the geographical locations of these events were important to the writers. Place names were carefully given, although in some instances the locations are not known. While in the Old Testament it may be the details of the battle, the ford, or the temple, in the New Testament, if the name is no longer current it is often a still-traceable road that points historians and archaeologists to the site.

Several other differences contrast the Old Testament with the New Testament: The Old Testament books are generally anonymous, and many had multiple authors. The New Testament books are identified by a single author (although the ascribed authorship of some is questioned). The Old Testament was written in Hebrew and Aramaic, and the experiences of the authors centered around the Hebrew people of Palestine. Much of the New Testament was written in a European language, Greek, and the writers of the majority of the books spent significant amounts of their lives in western Anatolia and Greece. The people of the Old Testament were rulers, prophets, and people of great substance. Eight towering Old Testament figures, possibly real only in poetic terms, are identified with Anatolia: Adam, Eve, Noah, Abraham, Sarah, Jacob, Rebecca, and Rachel. Those of the New Testament were itinerant preachers, trades people, and slaves. Nor is there much doubt that Paul and John really lived.

Questions of who wrote the books of the New Testament, when and where they were written, and why some books were included while others were not are even today entangled in theology and politics. The answers influence what we know about the early Church and its environment. Some were accepted because the right name was attached to them. Many 1st-and 2nd-century accounts were excluded because they were heretical Gnostic scriptures.

(The Gnostics emphasized intuitive knowledge and spiritual illumination—*gnosis*—while denying the material world. They also believed that knowing oneself deeply was being in touch with the divine. At this level they spoke of the mystery of such knowledge. This was in contradiction to orthodox belief that made a sharp distinction between the human and the divine. Paul himself was among those tainted with the charge of gnosticism, for instance when he admitted that his knowledge of Jesus came to him through a vision.)

With the discoveries of the Dead Sea Scrolls, some books that had been repressed when the biblical canon was established towards the end of the 4th century CE have resurfaced. They help add perspective to the picture of life and thinking in the early Christian community, with not only religious insights and aphorisms, with not only a wealth of apocalyptic writing (showing Revelation to have been a common 1st-century literary genre), but also with some rather inelegant details. Sentences from the apocryphal *Gospel of Philip* for instance, seem to parallel 1 Corinthians 13: "Faith receives, love gives. No one will be able to receive without love. No one will be able to give without love." *The Acts of Thomas* preaches the redemptive quality of virginity. The *Acts of John* recounts a night that the writer of Revelation and his friends were pestered by bedbugs. Among these books it would appear that the quantities and kinds of miracles that they recorded (the bedbugs obeyed John's order to leave the room) contributed to the reasons they were omitted.

In spite of the differences, like the Old Testament, the New Testament is concerned that God is revealed in people, in events, and in geographic locations. But while both sections of the Bible focus on the Word of God in human life, the New Testament is more concerned with the Christian message.

Jesus commissioned his apostles to go into all the world to preach the message he had given them. From Jerusalem they spread out, first among the Jewish communities nearby, then increasingly farther away. Of this initial dispersion, the largest known group took the message north from Palestine. As many as seven of the original twelve apostles can be counted working in Asia Minor if biblical accounts and legends are combined. According to Galatians (2:11), Peter was in Antioch for a time. The disciple John is thought by many to have been the author of the Book of Revelation, and to have returned to Ephesus after his exile on Patmos. The references to Matthew, Philip, Andrew, Thomas, and Thaddeus in Anatolia are not as conclusive. Paul's companions, Barnabas, John Mark, and Silas, although not among the Twelve, were presumably part of the original larger Jerusalem community of followers. Others who had not known Jesus during his lifetime soon joined the disciples, becoming leaders in the early church. Among these were Luke, Timothy, Lydia, Priscilla, Aquila, Philemon, Onesimus, Apollos, and Paul. Asia Minor was their testing ground.

The choice of Asia Minor came from a combination of family ties, proximity, welcoming reception, politics, geography, language, and religion. Each of these elements contributed to the development of Christianity.

Politics was the underlying force that directed events geographically. By the 1st century CE the focus of political power was no longer Babylon or Assyria to the east, but Rome to the northwest. Rome's control of its provinces required efficient communication with their resident governors. Therefore Rome developed and maintained a superb system of roads, many of them leading through Anatolia. While the shortest and possibly quickest routes to Rome were a combination of land and sea, the overland highways were somewhat more reliable than the sea, and offered more chances to the missionaries to meet people and do business. Weather, the seasons, and geography often operated together to affect the specific choices that travelers made.

The dominant languages were European, and that influenced the ease with which the western world understood the message. However, Rome's control did not extend to language: Regardless of the fact that the governing law was promulgated in Latin, the general populace spoke Greek with their friends. When they wanted to be remembered by posterity they carved Greek on their public buildings and tombstones. There were other languages, too. Many in southern Anatolia spoke Aramaic; the Jewish community knew Hebrew, and there were a few local pockets of other language groups such as the Lycaonians in Lystra. But Latin was never the everyday tongue in Anatolia.

Thus Paul, for instance, combined several advantages when he chose to travel into Asia Minor. As a Jew, he had entry into the synagogues wherever he went. He spoke both Hebrew and Greek, and maybe Aramaic as his mother tongue, so he could communicate his ideas fluently. His Roman citizenship gave him legal standing. Probably from his childhood in the port of Tarsus he had learned something about the Mediterranean coast, its cities and its peoples. He used religion, language, politics, and geography in his work. He called on his family background to show that he was a citizen of Rome and could claim its rights and privileges.

On the other hand, in fairness to the mission work that is not recorded in the New Testament, it must be noted that an increasing number of missionaries and their converts moved in the first century beyond the areas of Greek or Roman influence into Africa, eastern Anatolia, Russia, Persia, and India. These activities are less well-known and less credited in the West. The reasons are multiple. To some degree Western Christians are ignorant of this history because of the geographic remoteness of the Eastern Churches, to some because the languages used were Aramaic, or Armenian, or a host of others. To some degree the reasons are because the written records of the first missionaries outside of western Anatolia are not available. To some degree the beliefs and customs of these Christian communities differ from those that have been approved as orthodox by the Western Churches.

In this context, it should be recognized also that politics has played its part more than once in determining what is orthodox belief and what is heresy, in what will be reported and how, and in what will be suppressed. One early example of the place of politics is in the First Ecumenical Council in Nicaea (325 CE). Constantine the Great wanted to strengthen the power of his empire by identifying the state with a unified Christianity. Therefore he called representatives of all the churches to his palace and told them to write a single statement of belief. Most of the theologians were profoundly committed to finding words to express what is basically beyond words, and the Nicene Creed which they created is still used today. Even so, the question of which bishop's interpretation carried the most weight was answered often, not only then but in all the subsequent councils, on his standing in the community.

Barnabas

"Barnabas" was the nickname that the apostles in Jerusalem gave to their co-worker Joseph. Something in his character led them to call him this which meant "son of encouragement," or "son of exhortation." Although Joseph/Barnabas was well off, he chose to work with his hands. He was a leader; he was an example to the members of the early Church because he sold his estate and donated his money to the cause. When Saul/Paul was known only as a persecutor of the followers of Jesus, Barnabas courageously risked his reputation and the safety of the Jerusalem community by introducing him.

Barnabas was a Levite Jew from Cyprus. *When he came* [to Antioch] *and saw the grace of God, he rejoiced, and he exhorted them all to remain faithful to the Lord with steadfast devotion; for he was a good man, full of the Holy Spirit and of faith.* (Acts 11:23–24).

At the beginning of the Christian era, Antioch (Antakya), the capital of the Roman province of Syria, was a bustling center for commerce between Rome and the eastern world. Its residents were prosperous; they enjoyed themselves; and they were open to new ideas. In Antioch, Gentiles and Jews apparently mixed with fewer of the social restrictions than prevailed in Jerusalem. Gentiles were often drawn to Jewish practices because of the high ethical standards expected of the members. It was among this receptive community that Barnabas, who had been sent by the church in Jerusalem, began his work. Although before he arrived a small group of the followers of Jesus had been meeting in Antioch, Barnabas was the first missionary named in the New Testament in Anatolia.

Not only the first named, Barnabas was in charge of the first missionary journey through Anatolia. Even after the crowds in Lystra witnessed Paul's healing of a lame man, they assumed that Barnabas was the leader, the supreme god Jupiter, and that Paul was less important, merely his messenger Mercury. Perhaps Barnabas was the taller and appeared the more commanding of the two; he may also have been the older one. (Both Barnabas and Paul were horrified by that misapprehension of divinity. They reacted to it as blasphemy, and tore their clothes to avert a curse because, had they not done that, they would have been consenting to idolatry.)

When a difference occurred between Paul and Barnabas's cousin John Mark, Barnabas chose to support the young man. Barnabas and Paul parted company at the beginning of the second missionary journey; and none of his words, except as he and Paul spoke together, are recorded in the Bible. In the matter of contravening Jewish practice concerning associating with Gentiles at their meals, Barnabas sided with Peter instead of Paul (Gal. 2:11–14).

No known work exists that scholars accept as written by Barnabas; if such were found, it might answer some of the questions about early church practices, and about Paul's ministry and his personality. Certainly Barnabas could have added information that Luke did not know because Barnabas's acquaintance was of longer standing.

John Mark

The full identity of John Mark is uncertain. The references to John Mark may be to the same person as those to Mark, but there is no way to be sure. John Mark appeared in Acts first as a companion of Barnabas and Paul when they took relief supplies from Antioch to the famine victims in Jerusalem. He was a Jewish Christian resident in Jerusalem, a cousin of Barnabas. Presumably he was younger than the other two. His mother Mary was the head of the house to which Peter went when he found himself miraculously freed from prison. (Acts 13:5, 12:12)

On the first missionary journey, John Mark, Barnabas, and Paul started out from Antioch together, John Mark acting as their assistant. When they got as far as Perge he left them and returned to Jerusalem. No reason was given for his action.

The next time Paul wanted to go off as a missionary he disagreed with Barnabas over whether John Mark should accompany them or not. Barnabas evidently believed that his cousin had had a justifiable reason for returning to

Jerusalem, but Paul did not. Thus Barnabas and John Mark sailed to Cyprus a second time while Paul took Silas and started overland.

Mark, a cousin of Barnabas, is mentioned in the letter to the Colossians (Col. 4:10). That opens the questions of whether he is the same as John Mark, whether he and Paul had become friends again, or whether other references to Mark are also to him. (Phil. 24, 2 Tim. 4:11) A person by the name of Mark appears also in Peter's company in 1 Peter 5:13; by one tradition he is thought to be the same as Barnabas's cousin, and to have gone on to be Peter's interpreter after Paul died. Moreover, it has been claimed that Peter encouraged him to write what he had been taught about Jesus, and that what he wrote became the Gospel of Mark. Mark is supposed to have started the Church in Egypt, and—a later tradition—to have been buried in Venice. Mark is not an uncommon name, so it is easy to defend the possibility that each is a different person. The Bible does not answer these questions.

Luke

Luke has traditionally been identified as the author of both the Gospel of Luke and the Book of Acts. There is some question about whether this man was *"Luke, the beloved physician."* (Col. 4:14) In that same letter (4:11) Paul identified Mark, Barnabas, and Jesus Justus as Jewish Christians, leaving to inference the probability that Luke was a Gentile.

Scholars find that the points that the name "Luke," or in Latin "Lucius," was often a slave's name, and that likewise doctors were often slaves bring up questions about Luke's social standing. In relation to first century society, a high proportion of Christians were slaves. So, was Luke? When Paul speaks out for fair relations between slaves and their masters was he reflecting his attitude toward the way Luke had been treated?

> *Slaves, obey your earthly masters in everything, not only while being watched and in order to please them, but wholeheartedly, fearing the Lord. . . . Masters, treat your slaves justly and fairly, for you know that you also have a Master in heaven. (Col. 3:22, 4:1)*

Both the Gospel of Luke and the Book of Acts are thought to have been written between 80 and 90 CE. Chronologically the Book of Acts takes up where the Gospel leaves off, as though they are two parts of the same account. Scholars point out that the first fifteen chapters of Acts were written in the third person plural "they," while in Acts 16:10 the account changes to "we." They take that as evidence that the author was reporting what he had been told up to that point. From then on it is a first-hand report because, it is assumed, Luke joined Paul in Alexandria Troas just as they were sailing for Macedonia.

Luke apparently stayed in close contact with Paul through the rest of his journeys, being present in Greece, again in Troas, and on the trip that took Paul to Miletus and Jerusalem. He shared Paul's shipwreck on Malta and his arrival in Rome. If Luke was not actually present when Paul defended himself before the Court of Areopagus in Athens, he heard a detailed report of it, perhaps recounted to him by Paul himself, as may have happened also with Paul's address to the governor of Caesarea when Paul appealed to Caesar.

It may be difficult to reconstruct Paul's journeys exactly because Luke was specific only when he was physically with Paul. More to the point, Luke was concerned to give an account of Paul's work, not of their travels. The details about Paul that Luke does include, however, create a vivid picture of an inspired apostle whom he venerates. At the same time, Luke keeps himself always in the background.

A later tradition, perhaps going back only to the 6th century, describes Luke as an artist. According to it, several paintings of the Virgin Mary that have miraculous healing powers are considered by some to be his work. One of these is the "Black Virgin," a fresco on a wall of the Sumela Monastery in the mountains south of Trabzon.

Peter

Peter, the impetuous Galilean fisherman whom Jesus named "the rock," was a leader among the apostles in spreading the Gospel to the Gentile community outside the Jews of Palestine. While Paul is generally credited with Christianizing the West, Peter may have preceded him to Rome. His known writings are fewer than Paul's, but he is considered the founder of the Church in Rome and a less controversial figure than Paul. He was a liberal in his thinking: In the debate in Antioch and Jerusalem over who was eligible for membership in the Church, Peter, Barnabas, and Paul agreed that male circumcision was not to be a requirement.

However, later Paul scolded Peter openly for inconsistency:

> But when Cephas [Peter] came to Antioch, I opposed him to his face, because he stood self-condemned; for until certain people came from James, he used to eat with the Gentiles. But after they came, he drew back and kept himself separate for fear of the circumcision faction. And the other Jews joined him in his hypocrisy, so that even Barnabas was led astray by their hypocrisy. But when I saw that they were not acting consistently with the truth of the gospel, I said to Cephas before them all, "If you, though a Jew, live like a Gentile and not like a Jew, how can you compel the Gentiles to live like Jews?" (Gal. 2:11–14)

Peter stands out as a warmer, more approachable person than any of the other apostles. It is through his failings and his struggles to redeem himself that his humanity shines, most poignantly in his denial of Christ in Jerusalem. It is as he is transformed that he becomes Peter the Rock.

Two short letters carry his name in the New Testament, thought to have been written by him in Rome. They are 1st and 2nd Peter. He begins 1st Peter addressing the Christian communities in northern Anatolia, possibly reflecting his personal experience there:

To the exiles of the Dispersion in Pontus, Galatia, Cappadocia, Asia, and Bithynia who have been chosen and destined by God the Father and sanctified by the Spirit to be obedient to Jesus Christ and to be sprinkled with his blood: May grace and peace be yours in abundance. (1 Peter 1–2).

Tradition says that Peter visited Ankara (Galatia), but neither a physical remain nor a biblical reference is known to give color to that story. He is supposed to have died a martyr to his faith in Rome.

A legend concerning Peter and the early church in Antioch was made popular by the First Crusaders in the late 11th century. When they dug in a cave east of the city they found a sword that they claimed was the one with which Peter cut off the Roman centurion's ear in the Garden of Gethsemene. They said that this sword was in the cave because Peter had carried it there, and because the first Christians had used the cave for church meetings. Their find became a morale builder and a political weapon for these soldiers to use as they pressed on to Jerusalem.

The idea of the cave being the site of forbidden meetings is supported by a narrow tunnel that leads out the back of the cave and continues some distance away from the city. It is believed that the passage served as an escape route for Christians fleeing from their persecutors. Now Christian services are held openly in this Church of St. Peter.

Matthew

Three other apostles, Matthew, Philip, and Andrew, may have spent some time in Turkey, but there are no biblical references specifically substantiating this.

Church historians believe that the author of the Gospel of Matthew was a Jewish Christian who was resident in or near Antioch when he was writing. To support that, they point to the references in Matthew to insults, persecutions, and punishments that were common experiences there for Christians at the end of the 1st century (Matt.5:10–12; 10:17–18; 24:9–14). This bears out the tradition associated with the tunnel in the cave church in Antioch. There is a question about whether the same person was the apostle Matthew who was a tax collector (Matt.10:3). His name does not come up in any of the biblical books outside his gospel.

Philip

Likewise, the apostle Philip is associated with the early Church in Anatolia: According to the 4th-century church historian Eusebius, Philip lived in Hierapolis (near Laodicea), and at least one of his daughters lived in Ephesus. A number of first century Christian communities in Hierapolis and the surrounding area are evidenced by Paul's letters to the congregation in Colossae and to one of its members, Philemon, and by John's address to the church in Laodicea.

In recent years Italian archaeologists have uncovered and partially restored a building on the site of what is believed to be the burial place of Philip. It is on the hillside north of the baths in Hierapolis. They have not yet found the grave, nor is the building from the 1st century. A 5th-century CE structure, the floor plan is a square; a diagonal cross that defines a large, octagonal center cuts across the square. In its symmetry and simplicity it is one of the most pleasing early Byzantine buildings. While this is called a martyrium, implying that Philip was put to death for his belief, there is no record of such, nor has his body been found here.

What little there is in the Bible about Philip does not make a clear picture of the person, nor does the gnostic *Gospel of Philip*, one of the ancient Coptic texts found in Nag Hammadi in Egypt in the mid-20th century. However, a contemporary resident of Hierapolis, the Stoic philosopher Epictetas, described the ideal missionary as one who gave no thought to what he would wear or where he would sleep, but rather dedicated his life to returning love when he was persecuted for righteousness sake. One could hope that his picture might have been inspired by his acquaintance with Philip.

Andrew

Originally a disciple of John the Baptist, Andrew is considered the first missionary because he introduced his brother Simon Peter to Jesus. There is no biblical account of his later missionary work.

Andrew is held by the Eastern Orthodox Church (Greek Orthodox) to be its founder, thus identifying it as apostolic in origin. He is thought to have traveled through Byzantium (Constantinople, Istanbul) where he built a small chapel in today's Fındıklı before he continued on to the Baltic countries and to Scythia. He is supposed to have been buried in the no-longer-existing Church of the Holy Apostles in Constantinople.

Even without literary proof, there is firm evidence that Christians were active in Byzantium well before the reign of Constantine the Great. The present Church of St. Irene stands on foundations of a church building existing before Christianity was legal. Following the First Ecumenical Council in May of 325, Constantine took a number of churchmen with him to the small town of Byzantium to visit the bishop of that church. The bishop had been unable to attend the Council in Niceae because of his advanced age. Constantine's avowed purpose was to get the blessings of the leaders of the entire Church community for Byzantium to become the new capital of the Roman Empire.

Thomas and Thaddeus

Thomas and Thaddeus are two of the apostles named in the Gospels of Matthew and Mark. When Thomas asked to see the marks of the nails in Jesus' hands, he became the paradigm for those who demand concrete evidence before they can believe. The missionary work of neither man is noted in the New Testament, but the Armenian Orthodox and the Syrian Orthodox Churches hold that these men were instrumental in converting the first Christians in eastern Anatolia. By tradition, Thomas is credited with having pursued his work as far east as India where he is said to have baptized the daughter of a king. Tradition goes on to report that her father was so angered that he stabbed Thomas to death. Thereupon, a merchant from Edessa (Turkish Şanlıurfa) returned the body to his city where it was buried. There is no known grave today in Şanlıurfa marking Thomas' place of burial.

Another tradition, reported by the 4th-century church historian Eusebius, concerns King Abgar of Edessa who was suffering, perhaps from leprosy. (Western scholars doubt the historicity of this king.) King Abgar sent a letter asking Jesus to come heal him and offering Jesus refuge from his enemies. Eusebius says that Jesus replied regretting his inability to leave his responsibilities and thanking the king for his kind offer. Jesus promised eternal life and peace to all Abgar's people because of their belief in him. In his place Jesus sent Thaddeus who was so successful that he converted not only the king but also many of his subjects. Thus the Syrian Orthodox Church has claims not only to have been founded by an apostle, but also to date from before the crucifixion. Like Thomas, Thaddeus is said to have been buried in Şanlıurfa. The material that Eusebius had access to when he was compiling his Church history no longer exists, so the story remains unverified.

There are no known contemporary accounts of the missionary work of either Thomas or Thaddeus. Even so, the Syrian Orthodox Church is unquestionably one of the first, and its members still use Aramaic in their church services and in their daily lives. Even in the 21st century the life-style of the people living in the monasteries of Tur Abdin seems closer to that of Jesus' time than that of the people of Europe or America. Thus it is reasonable to agree that this branch of the Church has preserved traditions and practices of the early Christian community in their purity that the Western Church has forgotten.

The earliest record of missionary activity in eastern Turkey that is accepted in the West is that of the Christian writer, Tatian, who was active in the mid-2nd century. (Western theologians do not dispute the evidence that Christianity was established in the Syriac community before Tatian.) In about 175 CE Tatian contributed a "harmony" of the Gospels (called the *Diatessaron*) to the Syriac literature. The "harmony" was a compilation of the four Gospels into one book. This was so popular that it helped standardize the language.

Timothy

When he was a young man, Timothy was chosen by Paul to accompany him on his journeys. As he matured, he took on increasing independence and responsibilities for the missionary work. He and Paul met in his home of Lystra, a city not far from Iconium (see p. 80), the second time Paul was visiting there (Acts 16:1–10). In Paul's letter to the Corinthians he characterized the young man as *Timothy, who is my beloved and faithful child in the Lord* (1 Cor. 4:17).

Thanks to his Christian grandmother Lois, Timothy was a Christian before he met Paul. Although his mother and grandmother were Jewish, his father was not, and he was not circumcised until he became Paul's companion.

Timothy went with Paul and Silas to Thessaloniki and Corinth. Later he became Paul's messenger and interpreter. Paul's continuing regard for Timothy is evident in his letter to the Philippians:

> *I hope in the Lord Jesus to send Timothy to you soon, so that I may be cheered by news of you. I have no one like him who will be genuinely concerned for your welfare. . . . Timothy's worth you know, how like a son with a father he has served with me in the work of the gospel.* (Phil. 2:19–20, 22)

Lydia

A native of Thyatira (Akhisar) north of Smyrna, Lydia was living in Philippi when she met Paul. Philippi was a city in Macedonia on the main road, the Via Egnatia, between Rome and its eastern provinces. Its ruins are just west of today's Kavalla in northeastern Greece.

> *On the Sabbath day we* [Paul and Luke] *went outside the gate by the river, where we supposed there was a place of prayer; and we sat down and spoke to the women who had gathered there. A certain woman named Lydia, a worshiper of God, was listening to us; she was from the city of Thyatira and a dealer in purple cloth. The Lord opened her heart to listen eagerly to*

what was said by Paul. When she and her household were baptized, she urged us, saying, "If you have judged me to be faithful to the Lord, come and stay at my home." And she prevailed upon us. (Acts 16:13-15)

Among the points that are often inferred from this quotation are 1) that Lydia was converted almost as soon as Paul set foot in Europe—an omen of continuing success; 2) that she may have been a Gentile; 3) that not only was she well off, she was already a person of some prestige; and 4) that by including her household in this conversion she became a leader of a house church. Lydia welcomed the gift of Paul's message, and then welcomed the opportunity to return a gift of hospitality.

As a merchant of purple goods, Lydia was dealing in some of the most expensive and exclusive cloth—wool, silk, linen—then available. The purple dye she used came from relatively scarce salt-water snails found on the northeastern Mediterranean coast. Because it took many snails to produce a significant amount of dye, only the rich and the privileged wore purple cloth. It was made in a variety of shades, depending on the mordents used in the process. Purple as a mark of distinction is noted in other biblical contexts: The seat of Solomon's covered litter was of purple stuff (Song of Solomon 3:10), and the capable wife in Proverbs (31:22) wore purple. A stripe of Tyrian purple on a Roman toga identified a man as a member of the ruling class; by the 1st century BCE a complete robe of purple could be worn legally only by the emperor. Pilate's soldiers mockingly robed Jesus in purple just before he was crucified (Mat. 27:28). Purple continues its regal distinction: a son born to the reigning Byzantine emperor was "born in the purple" (*porphyrogenitus*), and an identification of a cardinal in the Catholic Church even today is his purple hat.

Lydia may not have been her real name; she may have been called this because she came from the general region of Lydian Sardis. Perhaps she had an important place in the Book of Acts because she was one of the first whom Paul baptized in Europe. (Another woman who is said to have been much influenced by Paul, Thecla, does not appear in the Bible.)

It was not unusual for women to be leaders at this time in some of the mystery cults such as the worship of Cybele, so her leadership of a home church would not necessarily make her stand out in the community. Likewise, at the same time many people had become disenchanted with paganism and were looking elsewhere for a focus of meaningful worship. Lydia may well have been ripe for conversion and have skillfully led her household in that search. Regrettably, there is no record of what happened to her after this encounter.

Priscilla and Aquila

Priscilla and Aquila were a couple who had considerable influence in the early Church. Paul acknowledged their importance in several passages.

After this [Paul's defense of Christianity in Athens] *Paul left Athens and went to Corinth. There he found a Jew named Aquila, a native of Pontus, who had recently come from Italy with his wife Priscilla, because Claudius had order all Jews to leave Rome. Paul went to see them, and, because he was of the same trade, he stayed with them, and they worked together—by trade they were tentmakers. (Acts 18:1–3)*

A year and a half later they accompanied Paul to Ephesus (Acts 18:11, 18) where they had a house church. Some time, some place during their acquaintance they rescued Paul from serious but unspecified danger. In writing about himself to the church members in Rome, Paul says, *Greet Prisca and Aquila, who work with me in Christ Jesus, and who risked their necks for my life, to whom not only I give thanks, but also all the churches of the Gentiles. (Rom. 16:3–4)*

It would appear from this that the order for Jews to vacate Rome had been rescinded, perhaps on the death of Claudius.

While Priscilla and Aquila were idealized for their generosity, scholars have wondered why she was usually mentioned first. Perhaps she had the stronger character and was the more outgoing of the two; perhaps she was educated, and the wealth they appear to have had was her property. Paul characterized her as one of his "co-workers," and, noticeably, did not suggest that she was subject to his authority.

Philemon and Onesimus

The letter by Paul to Philemon, written, it is thought, when Paul was in prison in Ephesus, is one of the most personal books of the Bible. Philemon was the head of a house church in Colossae (Phil. 2). The owner of at least one slave, a man named Onesimus, Philemon was well situated and able to support the Christian community. He may also have been a Roman citizen.

Onesimus seems to have run away from Philemon, either because Philemon mistreated him or because he had taken something from his owner. This slave's name and Paul's description of him involve a play on words: "Onesimus" in Greek meant "useful" or "profitable." Thus Paul wrote (paraphrasing verse 11): "*I appeal to you for Profitable, who was once profitless to you, but who now is profitable to both of us.*"

The reasons for the inclusion of this letter in the New Testament are not clear. It could be that, although the letter is very short, it raises the ethical questions of master-slave relations and responsibility. Probably, since it was preserved, Philemon did accept Onesimus back into his household. Beyond that, this Onesimus may have been the same man who became the bishop of Ephesus about sixty years later when the church leaders were beginning to decide on which writings that they possessed they should include in the canon of New Testament books. One other unanswerable question is whether, as Paul's very close friend, Onesimus was the author of the letter to the Ephesians, a letter which some scholars doubt was written by Paul himself.

Apollos

Apollos was a Jew who had been attracted to the teachings of Jesus from the little he had learned about him in Alexandria before he appeared in Ephesus. Befriended by Priscilla and Aquila, he grew in his understanding of Christianity under their guidance:

> Now there came to Ephesus a Jew named Apollos, a native of Alexandria. He was an eloquent man, well-versed in the scriptures. He had been instructed in the Way of the Lord; and he spoke with burning enthusiasm and taught accurately the things concerning Jesus, though he knew only the baptism of John. He began to speak boldly in the synagogue; but when Priscilla and Aquila heard him, they took him aside and explained the Way of God to him more accurately. (Acts 18:24–26)

Apollos went on from Ephesus to Corinth where he was involved in church leadership and thus became caught in a local quarrel. Judging from the account by Paul in 1 Corinthians, some members in Corinth had found Apollos' message more to their liking than Paul's. (Paul intended in 1 Corinthians to warn that church of the dangers of schism; he does not detail the points of difference between him and Apollos.) Apparently Apollos did not encourage the split; he was not interested in self-aggrandizement. He left Corinth before the quarrel was resolved, and, although the church invited him back, at the time of Paul's writing he did not intend to return soon. Paul summed up the situation, saying,

. . . as long as there is jealousy and quarreling among you, are you not of the flesh, and behaving according to human inclinations? For when one says, "I belong to Paul," and another, "I belong to Apollos," are you not merely human? What then is Apollos? What is Paul? Servants through whom you came to believe, as the Lord assigned to each. I planted, Apollos watered, but God gave the growth. (1 Cor. 3:3–6)

Other Followers

Among the names of almost 100 others who figure in the biblical accounts of the early missionary activities in Anatolia are Epaphras who founded a church in Colossae, Silas who took the place of Barnabas on Paul's second missionary journey, Alexander an apostate Christian who did Paul much evil, Gaius who was seized during the riot in Ephesus, Claudia who sent greetings to Timothy, Carpus who lived in Alexandria Troas, and Sosipater who was a Tarsian like Paul. Andronicus, a "kinsman" of Paul, was his fellow countryman; Nicholas was one of seven from Antioch chosen to minister to Greek-speaking Jews in Jerusalem; Zenas was a lawyer whom Paul asked to be sent somewhere with Apollos and taken good care of; Trophemus was a native of the Province of Asia. Nympha provided her house as one of the places of meeting for Christians in Colossae. (Philemon's home was one also.) The Church was a dynamic, versatile, very human body.

Paul the Disciple

More than for any other single missionary, it is what we know of Paul's activities, his writings, and his vision of what the Church should be that we trace how the Western world became Christianized.

Paul's Home

Paul began his life as a typical Jewish boy of the Dispersion in the Cilician town of Tarsus. The date of his birth is thought to have been about 10 CE. The name he was first known as was Saul; "Paul" was the Roman, not Jewish, name by which he became known after his encounter with Sergius Paulus, the Roman proconsul on Cyprus. (Acts 13:7–9)

Tarsus was an old city even in Paul's time. Its highest point, known locally as Gözlü Küle, was a mound of dirt that had accumulated on top of a Neolithic, and later a Bronze Age, settlement (c. 3000 BCE). Tarsus was under Hittite influence at the time of the Neo-Hittite, or Kizzuwatna, State (c. 1050–700 BCE). The Assyrian ruler Sennacherib sacked it in 696 BCE. Xenephon and the Persians were here in 400 BCE; he was impressed by its wealth. Alexander the Great stopped long enough in Tarsus (333 BCE) to swim in the river and catch what was almost his death of cold. When he did die in 323, the control of this part of his empire went to his general Seleucis Nicator.

While Paul may not have been interested in such by-gone times, he and his community would have had strong feelings against the Seleucid king Antiochus IV who followed Seleucis by about 150 years. In forcing Hellenism on the Jews and in building a pagan altar at the Temple in Jerusalem, Antiochus provoked the Maccabean revolt (167 BCE). (The Maccabeans were determined to keep Judaism pure.) It would seem likely that the Jews in Tarsus observed Hanukkah—the date that the Temple was cleansed of its pagan pollution—and that Paul was reminded of the story when he arrived as a student in Jerusalem. This conflict was not "ancient history" to him.

Even more recent for Paul's family was the plague of pirates that Tarsians suffered until the Roman general Pompey put an end to their activities in 67 BCE. (Pompey's purpose was to stop their raids on the grain shipments destined for Rome, not to redress the wrongs to Tarsus.) Following Pompey's operations, Cilicia, Syria, and Jerusalem came under Roman control (64 and 63 BCE). Twelve years later Cicero was resident in Tarsus as the governor of the province of Cilicia; during his term, Cicero was notable for his attempts to correct his predecessors' abuses of their office. Julius Caesar visited it in 47 BCE, and Mark Anthony was dazzled by Cleopatra in 41 BCE when she hove in sight in full regalia. Anthony removed some of the city's taxes, and a bit later Caesar Augustus gave it some commercial advantages. Paul's grandparents, and possibly his parents, could have witnessed these events.

Paul's home of Tarsus at the turn of the Christian Era (CE) was a busy, cosmopolitan port, with its opening to the Mediterranean through the lagoon at the mouth of the

Cydnus (Tarsus) River. Tarsus was at a crossroads of trade routes stretching between central Anatolia and the other Mediterranean ports. Its excellent harbor and its surrounding roads served to keep the business growing here. The Emperor Justinian thought he was doing the city a favor in the 6th century CE when he changed the course of the river to alleviate its flooding (a recurring problem up to today). Instead, the river stopped flushing out the lagoon. Thus, the harbor and its sea traffic are no more, and the coast slopes gently into the distant Mediterranean 15 km to the south.

Looking at Paul from today's world when communications are both instantaneous and worldwide, it is hard for us to imagine that an alert young man like him would not have been cognizant of currents of thought outside his religious community. Instead, many scholars dismiss any significant influence of Gentile thought on early Christianity. The one point at which it may have had some influence on Paul is in the contemporary popular Stoic philosophy. The most obvious reason for suggesting this is because Tarsus was the location of a distinguished university with such resident teachers as the Stoic Athenodorus Cananites who was a close associate of Cicero and Caesar Augustus. Its citizens shared with Rhodes, Alexandria, and Athens the pride of internationally recognized scholarly pursuits. Perhaps there are traces of Stoic thought in Paul's phrase that *man's existence is in God* (1 Cor. 13:12). (The Stoics equated truth with freedom, and ignorance with slavery, a thought that echoes in the phrase from John 8:32: *and the truth will make you free.*) Another point of contact was the Stoic and

Epicurean philosophers who joined issue with Paul in Athens, calling on him to defend his views before the Court of Aeropagus (Acts 17:16-34). Later, Stoicism had an important influence on the 3rd-century Christian theologians Tertullian and Origen.

Paul's Family and Education

Paul must have gotten the standard religious education of a Jewish boy in the Tarsus synagogue. His mother tongue probably was Aramaic or Greek, but he would have learned Hebrew in the synagogue. He would have studied the Old Testament scriptures, perhaps at first in a Septuagint (Greek translation) version. Early on he must have shown an exceptional aptitude and eagerness for such learning. Perhaps he picked up a smattering of other languages that were shouted around the harbor. From his father he learned the trade of making tents and the associated leatherworking.

With the expectation that Paul could become a distinguished rabbi (teacher, judge), he was sent to Jerusalem for advanced studies. His parents naturally would have been proud of him and told him many times that he would bring honor to his family and to his tribe. Some of the intensity of his personality could have been a family trait.

The leading rabbi in Jerusalem at the time was the Pharisee, Gamaliel. If not the grandson of the hermeneutics scholar Rabbi Hillel (as it was once claimed), Gamaliel followed closely in Hillel's tradition of piety tempered by charity. Several of the sentences attributed to Hillel have parallels in the Gospels and in Paul's writings: "Don't judge another until you are in his position" ("*Do not judge, so that you may not be judged. For with the judgment you make you will be judged, and the measure you give will be the measure you get.*" Matt. 7:1–2). "That which you would consider unpleasant, do not do to your neighbor: this is not only the Law, but its entire meaning" (*For the whole law is summed up in a single commandment, "You shall love your neighbor as yourself."* Gal. 5:14).

Gamaliel was looked up to because of his learning and his tempered thinking in a crisis. At the time when the followers of Jesus in Jerusalem were attracting much attention in the temple, the members of the Jewish council, the Sanhedrin, wished to put them to death for preaching about Christ's resurrection and his message of salvation. Gamaliel argued against their desire:

> *When they heard this, they were enraged and wanted to kill them* [the followers]. *But a Pharisee in the council named Gamaliel, a teacher of the law, respected by all the people, stood up and ordered the men to be put outside for a short time. Then he said to them, "Fellow Israelites, consider carefully what you propose to do with these men. . . . I tell you, keep away from these men and let them alone; because if this plan or this undertaking is of human origin, it will fail; but if it is of God, you will not be able to overthrow them—in that case you may even be found fighting against God!"* (Acts 5: 33–39 passim)

It is thought that Paul arrived in Jerusalem after the crucifixion of Jesus, about 32 or 33 CE, where his teacher was this same Gamaliel. By his own admission, he was present at and approved of the stoning of Stephen (Acts 22:20); stoning was the form of capital punishment prescribed by Jewish law for the crime of blasphemy. (Crucifixion was a Roman, not a Jewish, punishment.)

The Conversion

Continuing his harassment of the followers of Jesus, Paul set off to persecute them in Damascus. As he approached the city he was blinded by his vision of Jesus (Acts 9:2-5). From persecutor Paul turned to missionary, one who dedicated his life to fulfilling the responsibilities of this vision. Upon his own conversion, he spent some time in Damascus, Arabia, and again in Jerusalem. In both Damascus and Jerusalem his zeal put him in physical danger and he had to flee for his life. Scholars estimate that this was sometime between 34 and 37 CE when Paul was about 25 years old.

Paul returned to Tarsus. One would suppose that he was living at home then and that he might have gone back to practicing his trade of tent making with his father. At the same time, one might also wonder how warmly this convert was welcomed by the members of the Tarsus synagogue. Judging by his later career, it would seem likely that he did not stay silent or inactive for long. About 37 or 38 CE his friend from Jerusalem sought him out:

Mt. Ararat

Euphrates River

Harran

Harran: traditional "beehive" houses

Anna Edmonds

Tarsus: St. Paul's Gate

Archaeology and Art Publications

Tarsus: St. Paul's Well

Anna Edmonds

Hierapolis: Martyrium of St. Philip

Archaeology and Art Publications

Antioch

Pisidian Antioch

Alexander Troas, with the Aegean Sea in the background

Perga (Perge)

Ephesus (Efes)

Ephesus: Temple of Hadrian

*Selçuk: baptistry
in the Cathedral of
St. John the Theologian*

House of the Virgin Mary near Ephesus

Smyrna (Izmir): market square

Thyatira (Akhisar)

Pergamum (Bergama): Temple of Zeus and the Bergama plain

Sardis (Sart): Temple of Artemis

Sardis: decoration in a 3rd-century synagogue

Philadelphia (Alaşehir): 11th-century church

Laodicea (Laodikya): ruins of a public fountain

Then Barnabas went to Tarsus to look for Saul, and when he had found him, he brought him to Antioch. So it was that for an entire year they met with the church and taught a great many people, and it was in Antioch that the disciples were first called Christians. (Acts 11:25-26)

Paul the Preacher

For more than twenty years Paul labored as an itinerant minister, indefatigable in his zeal to preach God's grace and righteousness. He traveled extensively throughout the eastern Mediterranean, braving disease and imprisonment, criticism from his closest associates and the disappointment of seeing his converts becoming apostates, yet always carrying his assured vision that neither death nor life could separate Christians from the love of God revealed in Jesus.

Paul's Journeys

Over a period of about ten to fifteen years, Paul traveled several times back and forth in western Anatolia, stopping for memorable encounters in Pisidian Antioch, Iconium, Lystra, Alexandria Troas, Ephesus, and Miletus. Other cities are mentioned along the way, and general regions are mentioned, but the reader is often left to wonder just what routes Paul took to get from one place to the next.

Several reasons could be suggested for Paul's various routes through Anatolia: The places associated with Paul are, for the most part, major cities like Iconium, Miletus, and Perge. There he would have found already established Jewish communities. The people whom Paul or his associates knew in a particular place might have drawn him. Perhaps Paul journeyed to Pisidian Antioch because his associates in Antioch-on-the-Orontes had family or friends there. He might have chosen the best roads, or taken the transportation that was available when he was ready to move. Paul may have turned away from entering Bithynia on his second journey because of road conditions. (Or perhaps some kind of reported disturbance. Or a premonition.) When he chose to go overland to Assos he may have wanted that chance to visit with friends who were traveling that direction. The time of year and the weather must have had some influence: People preferred to travel during the late spring and the summer months. Paul probably journeyed overland rather than by ship from Ephesus to Macedonia after the riot in the theater because the winter season was approaching and the sea could be unpredictable. Along with these possibilities, he acknowledged that visions and dreams at times had bearing on his actions: His decisions to go to Macedonia and to Rome he attributed to the visions he saw.

Some references in Acts appear to be contradicted by other references in the Letters: Did Paul interrupt his stay in Ephesus to make a hasty, painful trip to Corinth (2 Cor. 2:1)? Some references seem to confuse the sequence of events: Did Paul attend the conference in Jerusalem near the beginning of his ministry (Acts 15:4–21), or near the end (Gal 2:1–10)? Were there two conferences? These questions, however, are insignificant in relation to the impact he made on those who heard his message.

At the beginning of his missionary work and when he arrived in a new city Paul went first to the synagogue. Only after his message had been rejected by the Jewish community did he turn his attention more purposefully to the Gentiles. He concentrated on large cities where not only there must have been numbers of resident Jews, but also where there were Gentiles searching for meaning beyond the current mythology or the Oriental mystic cults.

Descriptions of Paul's journeys are usually based on the account in Acts that seems to detail three separate trips. The first one is relatively easy to follow: Paul, Barnabas, and Barnabas' nephew John Mark sailed from Seleucia Pieria to Cyprus (Salamis, Paphos) and then back to the mainland at Perge (a port on the Cestrus/Aksu River a short distance upstream from the coast). Paul and Barnabas went from Perge to Pisidian Antioch, to Iconium, to Lystra and Derbe, back through Iconium and Pisidian Antioch, and then returned by sea from Attalia to Antioch-on-the-Orontes (Acts 13, 14). The trip probably filled up their summer and early fall.

The second journey took Paul overland through Syria (Antioch was part of the province of Syria) and Cilicia to Lystra and Derbe, from town to town in Phrygia and Galatia, skirting the province of Asia, northwards toward Bithynia, and west through Mysia to the port of Alexandria Troas. From there Paul and Luke (who had joined him in

Alexandria Troas) sailed to Samothrace and continued on to Neapolis, Philippi, Amphipolis, Apollonia, Thessalonica, Beroea, Athens, Corinth, Cenchreae, back to Ephesus, on to Caesarea Maritima, Jerusalem, and at last again Antioch (Acts 15:36–18:22).

On the third journey, Paul started from Antioch traveling through Galatia and Phrygia to Ephesus. After two or three years he went to Macedonia and Greece, then came back to Alexandria Troas, Assos, Mitylene, Samos, Miletus, Cos, Rhodes, Patara, Tyre, and Jerusalem. (Acts 18:23–21:17)

When Paul was en route to Rome, he sailed from Sidon, skirted Cyprus, and landed in Myra. From there the ship sailed north towards Cnidus, then turned west to Crete. He was shipwrecked on Malta, but eventually reached Rome sometime before 62 CE.

Antioch-on-the-Orontes

Antioch-on-the-Orontes (Antakya) was the location of Paul's home church during the time of his missionary travels. Golden Antioch, capital of the Roman province of Syria, had a population of close to half a million people when Paul arrived there with Barnabas around 38 CE. The history of the city had started with its founding in about 300 BCE by Alexander the Great's general, Seleucis Nicator. Then in 64 BCE Antioch became a part of the Roman Empire when Pompey organized the province of Syria with it as the capital. Its Roman governors favored it; Julius

Caesar confirmed its status as a free city, and subsequent emperors contributed to its public buildings. But while it was the capital, its port was about 30 km away at Seleucia Pieria on the coast because rapids in the Orontes River half way down stream made it unnavigable. When Paul took ship from Antioch it was from this Seleucia Pieria that he sailed.

Antioch was the third largest city in the Roman Empire, smaller and less important only than Rome and Alexandria. The Antiochenes probably aped many of the ways of Rome, perhaps being even more liberal-minded than the Romans themselves. They were as eager to have their city an up-to-date metropolis as any city dweller is today. In keeping with the political climate of the times, Antioch looked west, not east, to determine its standards.

The most desirable residential suburb of Antioch was Daphne, now a favored picnic spot 10 km to the southwest. Daphne was a wooded hillside where ribbons of white water coursing through the trees made it a pleasantly cool park in the heat of summer. Legend had it that this was where the nymph Daphne had been saved from Apollo's advances when Zeus changed her into a bay tree. Seleucis, the founder of Antioch, honored the god as the leader of the Muses with a statue to him in the temple to Apollo in Daphne.

The Roman villas of Daphne were sumptuously decorated, their floors and walls covered with large mosaics, now displayed in the Hatay Museum in Antioch. These illustrate intricate scenes from mythology (Hercules, Perseus, and

75

Andromeda with a fantastically horrid beast, Orpheus surrounded by listening animals), some humorous scenes from real life (a happy hunchback, a sundial with the indication that the time for work is past), and portraits, possibly of the owners. They show the grace and technical skills of the artists who worked with the unyielding medium of tiny tesserae. They also are a comment on the licentious, sybaritic life for which Daphne attracted much notoriety.

Antioch, rather than Jerusalem, was the city which Paul and his companions considered their home base and from which they set out on their journeys north through Anatolia and into Europe. Antioch remained the center to which they returned. Perhaps the Antiochenes were more tolerant of missionary work among Gentiles than the Jewish community of Jerusalem; perhaps their attitudes and their contacts with people in the commercial centers around Anatolia were important influences in the next moves that Paul made. The Christians of Antioch quickly took a leading role in church development; later more than thirty church councils were held there. Even now the titular seats of three Catholic patriarchs in Antioch (Syrian, Maronite, and Greek Melchite) and two Eastern patriarchs (Greek Orthodox and Syrian Orthodox) recognize this history.

Perga

Perga in Pamphylia (Perge) was the port of entry to Anatolia for Barnabas, John Mark, and Paul on their first missionary journey. (Acts 13:13) It was comfortably located near the

Cestrus (Aksu) River that gave access to the sea but distance enough to protect them from pirates, and was close enough to the Taurus (Toros) mountains so that residents could escape to them during the heat of summer. It had a central acropolis that with its fortifications on top helped protect the city, and that with its theater cradled on the eastern slope offered them entertainment.

An attractive city with many stately public buildings, the residents believed that Perga had been founded by Greek soldiers after the Trojan war. A bronze tablet found at the Hittite city of Boğazkale in 1968 recorded in cuneiform a treaty between King Tuthalya IV (1250–1220 BCE) and King Kuruata of Tarhuntassa; Tarhuntassa has been identified as Perga. The word "Perga" perhaps came from an ancient goddess, a not uncommon source of proper names.

Of the buildings now visible in Perga, the theater and the stadium are those that most visitors see first. The horseshoe court of the city gate and the southern baths were not there when Paul arrived, but he would have noted the colonnaded avenue with its central stepped water course. Much of the statuary found by archaeologists in Perge is exhibited in the museum in Antalya, including one of Plancia Magna, the woman who was a major benefactor and civic leader in the early 2nd century CE.

Paul seems to have spent little time in the city on his first visit. On his return, as he was getting ready to sail for Antioch, he and Barnabas stopped long enough to give their message to its citizens:

> *. . . they passed through Pisidia and came to*
> *Pamphylia. When they had spoken the word in Perga,*
> *they went down to Attalia* [Antalya]. *From there they*
> *sailed back to Antioch.* (Acts 14:24–25)

Pisidian Antioch

Pisidian Antioch was situated on a slope of the Sultan Dağları range just west of modern Yalvaç. This Antioch seems to have been founded about 270 BCE by Antiochus I Soter, son and successor to his murdered father Seleucis Nicator. He colonized it with people whom he moved from Magnesia-on-the-Meander. Like Rome, this Antioch covered the slopes of seven hills. The population of the area in Paul's time may have been as many as 100,000 people.

According to the excavations still being carried out by Turkish and foreign archaeologists, the walls of Antioch enclosed a relatively small area. The western entrance was through a handsome triple gateway with symbols of the winged goddess of Victory holding garlands over the arches. Close by was the theater. Of the other major buildings that have been identified, one was a temple to Caesar Augustus, another a square in honor of Tiberius, one was a public fountain, one a bath, and one perhaps the city council chamber. Two wide, paved streets ran through the city at right angles to each other. The stones in the colonnaded main street are rutted from much use. The temple to Augustus is on the high point of the city; fragments of Augustus' deeds, the *Res Gestae*, were found here in 1912. While the official language of Antioch was Latin, its residents spoke Greek, a duality reflected in the Greek inscriptions on the tombstones, but in the Latin that recorded what Augustus wanted to be remembered for. There was a substantial Jewish community resident when Paul arrived.

Inside the city, but near the wall are the ruins of the large basilical church of St. Paul, built during Byzantine times. It replaced an earlier synagogue.

An ancient 10-kilometer aqueduct that brought water to the city from the Sultan Dağları came in from the north. Between 5 and 7 meters tall, about 250 meters of it are still standing. Constructed of ashlar, the stones were so perfectly cut that they needed no mortar to bind them together.

Upon their arrival in Pisidian Antioch, Paul and Barnabas went to the Sabbath service in the synagogue. At the appropriate time in the service they were asked if they had anything to urge upon the congregation. Paul rose and gave his first recorded sermon:

> *You Israelites, and others who fear God, listen. The God of this people Israel chose our ancestors and made the people great during their stay in the land of Egypt, and with uplifted arm he led them out of it. . . . My brothers, you descendants of Abraham's family, and others who fear God, to us the message of this salvation has been sent. . . . David, after he had served the purpose of God in his own generation, died, was laid beside his ancestors, and experienced corruption; but he whom God raised up experienced no corruption. Let it be known to you therefore, my brothers, that through*

this man forgiveness of sins is proclaimed to you. . .
(Acts 13:16–38 passim)

Paul aroused enough interest in those who heard him that he and Barnabas were asked to return the next Sabbath. In the interim, the interest grew to such an extent that, the account says, *almost the whole city gathered to hear the word of the Lord* (Acts 13:44).

Many of those attending the second Sabbath service were not members of the synagogue. It is understandable that Paul and Barnabas were pleased to have drawn so much attention, and with their experience in Antioch-on-the-Orontes behind them they welcomed the involvement of the Gentiles.

However, it is also understandable that the Jewish congregation was disturbed by the outsiders (who may not have known how to behave in a synagogue), and wanted to protect the sanctity of their place of worship. Among those who disapproved of what the two missionaries had done were some important Jewish women. They complained to the city officials and together forced Paul and Barnabas to leave town.

Iconium

From Pisidian Antioch, Paul and Barnabas moved southeast to Iconium (Konya). Iconium sat in a fertile agricultural basin known for its gardens and orchards that were watered by streams from the mountains to the north. It probably was a large city, and many of its residents well off.

The missionaries arrived in Iconium soon after they had been expelled from Antioch. Here they continued their preaching. Some of those for whom the religion of their fathers was stale found the message that Barnabas and Paul brought a welcome challenge. For others its power was disturbing.

The same thing occurred in Iconium, where Paul and Barnabas went into the Jewish synagogue and spoke in such a way that a great number of both Jews and Greeks became believers.

> But the unbelieving Jews stirred up the Gentiles and poisoned their minds against the brothers. So they remained for a long time, speaking boldly for the Lord, who testified to the word of his grace by granting signs and wonders to be done through them. But the residents of the city were divided, some sided with the Jews, and some with the apostles. And when an attempt was made by both Gentiles and Jews, with their rulers, to mistreat them and to stone them the apostles learned of it and fled to Lystra and Derbe, cities of Lycaonia, and to the surrounding country, and there they continued proclaiming the good news. (Acts 14:1–7)

Thecla

An apocryphal story about Paul in Iconium is contained in the very popular 2nd-century work called *The Acts of Paul and Thecla*. Thecla was an adolescent daughter of an illustrious family in Iconium. Although she was engaged to be married, she was strongly attracted to Paul and his message, and sought him out for his counsel. Paul was not romantically attracted to her. Against the commands of her parents, she became a Christian. Her determination to follow Paul's teachings was such that she was willing to be a celibate missionary of the Gospel. Thoroughly disgusted by their daughter's choice, her parents and the city officials condemned her to the stake, but when the fire was lit, a timely rain extinguished the flames. Later she was thrown to the wild animals, but from each danger she escaped unscathed. At one point, to protect herself and escape from an unwanted advance, she cut off her hair and dressed in men's clothing. Paul found it hard to believe her until her persistence won him over and he blessed her calling. With that, she went on to found a nunnery that for several hundred years was famous for its medical care. The ruins of her nunnery and a 5th-century CE basilica named for her are near the Mediterranean coast southwest of Silifke.

A number of similar stories celebrating the miracles of the disciples and their followers were current in the 2nd and 3rd centuries. The pulp fiction of the time, they contained about as much truth as their modern counterparts. The continuing interest in this story about St. Thecla is partly because it may give a fairly accurate picture of Paul: In it Paul is described as short in stature, knock-kneed but with good-looking legs, bald, hollow-eyed, and crooked-nosed. He was *"full of grace, for sometimes he appeared as a man, sometimes he had the countenance of an angel."*

Today's Konya is a place of religious pilgrimage for both Christians and Muslims. During the 12th to 14th centuries CE Iconium was the center of the Muslim Seljuk Empire. Buildings of the schools of Islamic theology, such as the Karatay Medresesi, the Inci Minareli Medrese and the Sirçali Medrese, are examples of Seljuk artistry. It was also during this period that the mystic Celaleddin Rumi (Jelal ed-din ar-Rumi) (d. 1273) lived in Konya. The impress of his teachings and that of his followers, the Mevlevi Dervishes, have made Konya a holy place for Muslims ever since.

Lystra, Derbe

The locations of Lystra and Derbe are not known for certain. Stones inscribed with the names of these two cities are in the Konya museum, but exactly where the stones came from originally no one knows. What can be deduced from the Bible is that Derbe and Lystra were somewhere near Iconium and in the region of Lycaonia, perhaps on the border between it and the province of Galatia. Few contemporary records exist that could help identify either city, nor are the boundaries of the provinces at the time known; thus most of what biblical archaeologists have to rely on is the reasonableness of where Paul and Barnabas would have found safety. Thus Hatunsaray, Ilistra, Madenşehri, or Bin Bir Kilise could be acceptable, or any of a number of other locations in the Konya plain.

For instance, Hatunsaray, about 25 km south of Konya, has some claim to be Lystra, but nothing has been found to confirm the identification. Hatunsaray is a small village. Another possibility is in the name of the village of Ilıstra which is farther south. A third town suggested sometimes is Madenşehri north of Karaman.

A neighbor of Madenşehri, the village of Bin Bir Kilise, otherwise called Değle, holds some interest as the possible location of Derbe. The name of this place translates to mean "A Thousand and One Churches." Without question the ruins of many, many churches are concentrated in this small mountain hideout. While there are evidences that people have lived here since the Hittites in the 2nd millennium BCE, the several ruined Christian churches do not appear to be earlier than 5th century CE. That date in itself does not rule out the possibility of a community that could have welcomed Paul. Certainly in the first century people would not have wanted to attract the wrath of Rome with a building openly defying the worship of the State. So homes rather than churches would have been the option for meeting places until Christianity was legalized in the 4th century.

William Ramsay, a New Testament scholar, spent much effort at the turn of the 20th century trying to identify the Roman roads that Paul would logically have followed in his journeys through Anatolia. He looked for and found some of the Roman milestones, some parts of the roads themselves, and parts of the boundaries of the Roman provinces. However, even with his careful, detailed study, many questions such as these about Lystra and Derbe remain.

Because Paul apparently understood the shouts of the people when he healed a lame man in Lystra, it is possible that he knew some of the local Lycaonian language.

At Lystra there was a man sitting who could not use his feet and had never walked, for he had been crippled from birth. He listened to Paul as he was speaking. And Paul, looking at him intently and seeing that he had faith to be healed, said in a loud voice, "Stand upright on your feet." And the man sprang up and began to walk. When the crowds saw what Paul had done, they shouted in the Lycaonian language, "The gods have come down to us in human form!" Barnabas they called Zeus, and Paul they called Hermes, because he was the chief speaker. The priest of Zeus, whose temple was just outside the city, brought oxen and garlands to the gates; he and the crowds wanted to offer sacrifice. When the apostles Barnabas and Paul heard of it, they tore their clothes and rushed out into the crowd shouting, "Friends, why are you doing this? We are mortals just like you, and we bring you good news, that you should turn from these worthless things to the living God, who made the heaven and the earth and the sea and all that is in them. . . ." Even with these words they scarcely restrained the crowds from offering sacrifices to them. But Jews came there from Antioch and Iconium and won over the crowds. They stoned Paul, and dragged him out of the city, supposing that he was dead. But when the disciples surrounded him, he got up and went into the city. The next day he went on with Barnabas to Derbe. (Acts 14:8-15, 18-20)

It would appear from the account in Acts and from their later journeys that Paul and Barnabas were not discouraged by such attacks, but rather considered their first missionary attempts successful.

The Second and Third Journeys

On Paul's second missionary journey he went with Silas back through Syria and Cilicia (possibly stopping en route in Tarsus) to Lystra, possibly continuing north from Tarsus through the Cilician Gates (Gülek Boğazı) or on southwest following the coast to Silifke and then up the Calycadnus (Göksu) River to the high, central plain. These were the two common, most direct roads into the interior. They were not the only options, but the other routes would have taken them out of their way to no obvious purpose.

In spite of having been almost killed in Lystra, Paul made no issue of the courage it must have taken him to risk his life there again. It was on this visit that he found Timothy who from then on became his youthful companion.

The route that Paul took from Lystra is unclear; only the regions are noted:

> They went through the region of Phrygia and Galatia, having been forbidden by the Holy Spirit to speak the word in Asia. When they had come opposite Mysia, they attempted to go into Bithynia, but the Spirit of Jesus did not allow them; so, passing by Mysia, they went down to Troas. (Acts 16:6–8)

Galatia, Cappadocia

There is a tradition that Paul (or Peter) founded the church in Angora (Ankara), a major city in Galatia. In his letter to the Galatians Paul thanks them:

> . . . *You know that it was because of a physical infirmity that I first announced the gospel to you; though my condition put you to the test, you did not scorn or despise me, but welcomed me as an angel of God, as Christ Jesus.* (Gal. 4:13-14)

The reference has left scholars puzzled over what he meant. Did he visit them in person, and if so where was he in Galatia? Part of the puzzle comes from the borders of Galatia being unknown. Many have felt that Ankara was too far away from any of the named cities for Paul ever to have gotten there.

However, if he did get to Ankara, he may have also traveled into Cappadocia. The remote valleys of Göreme, Soğanlı, and Ihlara and the troglodyte churches there invite comparisons with 1st-century CE life. Or, since he skirted the province of Asia, he may have followed the main road from Lystra and Iconium that went west through Pessinus (Ballıhisar near Sivrihisar) to Dorylaeum (Eskişehir) where he tried to enter Bithynia. From there he could have turned southwest through Cotyaeum (Kütahya) and gone on to the Aegean coast. Whatever route he took, it was a long, dusty journey. Other than tradition, wishful speculation, and the evidence that Paul never stinted himself, there is no known basis for any specific claim for any one of these routes. However, by the 3rd century CE at least one Christian community was active in Philomelium (Akşehir); concerning the martyrdom of Bishop Polycarp (c. 156 CE), they sent to Smyrna to ask for an accounting of the event. By the early 4th century, Cappadocia was home to several important Christian theologians, among them Basil the Great.

Alexandria Troas

Alexandria Troas was a seaport on the Aegean, founded about 310 BCE, and named both for Alexander the Great and for the geographic region of the Troad. Its importance declined rapidly after Constantine the Great chose Byzantium (Constantinople, Istanbul) to become the capital of the Eastern Roman Empire in 330 CE. That he plundered the buildings of Troas to build his new city did not improve its fortunes. However, by then Troas was largely deserted, providing Constantine with a quantity of unclaimed and already dressed stones. Such plunder continued into the Ottoman period; very little is visible today of the old port other than the remains of the 2nd-century CE Herodes Atticus Baths, many potsherds, and the outline of the harbor.

While its location gave it a strategic importance in controlling and taxing the traffic through the Hellespont (Çanakkale Boğazı) during its brief existence, its harbor was artificial and could be defended only with difficulty. Alexandria Troas profitted from the busy trade routes between the Black Sea, the Aegean, and the Mediterranean. In its heyday it may have had a population of 100,000 people.

Paul arrived in Alexandria Troas, perhaps in the middle of summer, probably hot and tired from the trip. Almost at once he had a vision of an opportunity for missionary work across the sea in Greece. This is counted by church historians to be the beginning of the evangelization of Europe and the West. It is the first record in the Bible of anyone reaching out beyond the Middle East.

> *During the night* [in Troas] *Paul had a vision: there stood a man of Macedonia pleading with him and saying, "Come over to Macedonia and help us." When he had seen the vision, we immediately tried to cross over to Macedonia, being convinced that God had called us to proclaim the good news to them.*

> *We set sail from Troas and took a straight course to Samothrace, the following day to Neapolis, and from there to Philippi, which is a leading city of the district of Macedonia and a Roman colony.* (Acts 16:9–12)

Paul returned to Troas near the end of his third journey after he had spent three months in Greece. He was in a hurry to get to Jerusalem in time for Pentecost (so this could have been in late April or May), but he stayed in Troas a week talking with his friends.

The Saturday night before he and his companions left, they were all gathered in an upstairs room to finish their visit, to hear Paul's message one more time, to celebrate the Eucharist, and to say good-by. Perhaps it was a warm spring night; even though the windows were open, the room became stuffy from all the people present and the many burning lamps.

> *A young man named Eutychus, who was sitting on the window, began to sink off into a deep sleep while Paul talked still longer. Overcome by sleep, he fell to the ground three floors below and was picked up dead. But Paul went down, and bending over him took him in his arms, and said, "Do not be alarmed, for his life is in him." Then Paul went upstairs, and after he had broken bread and eaten, he continued to converse with them until dawn; then he left. Meanwhile they had taken the boy away alive and were not a little comforted.* (Acts 20:9-12)

There is an interesting detail about a cloak in Paul's second letter to Timothy: "*When you come, bring the cloak that I left with Carpus at Troas, also the books, and above all the parchments.*" (2 Tim. 4:13) Maybe Paul had covered Eutychus with his cloak to protect him against the shock of the fall, and forgot it when he left the next morning. Maybe the boy was sleeping and Paul did not want to disturb him to get his cloak and his books.

On the southern coast of the Troad peninsula and within easy view of the island of Mitylene was another busy port, that of Assos (Behramkale). Paul traveled overland to Assos when he left Troas after his all-night conversation. There he met his friends who had taken a ship from Troas, and they continued south, stopping briefly at Mitylene and then at Miletus.

Paul in Ephesus

Paul made at least two visits to Ephesus (Efes). The first time he was headed from Corinth for Syria and Jerusalem at the end of his second journey, he stopped in Ephesus en route:

> *After staying there* [in Corinth] *for a considerable time, Paul said farewell to the believers and sailed for Syria, accompanied by Priscilla and Aquila. At Cenchreae he had his hair cut, for he was under a vow. When they reached Ephesus, he left them there, but first he himself went into the synagogue and had a discussion with the Jews. When they asked him to stay longer, he declined, but on taking leave of them, he said, "I will return to you, if God wills." Then he set sail from Ephesus.* (Acts 18:18–21)

After that visit to Jerusalem, Paul returned through Galatia and Phrygia to Ephesus. The details of his stops along the route are missing; perhaps he was hastening to Ephesus because of the previous invitation he had had; perhaps he was concerned about the reports he had gotten from Priscilla and Aquila about the activities of Apollos in the synagogue there (see p. 63).

This second visit for Paul lasted more than two years, perhaps from about 53 to 55 CE. Paul by this time was an experienced preacher, having worked as such for fifteen or sixteen years.

Ephesus was a major port city at the mouth of the Cayster River. Once located on the open sea, by Paul's time the city's harbor was a lagoon. Its coast was some ways off, having been pushed away by the debris that the river was depositing in the delta. Eventually the city lost the struggle against the river that still pushes the coastline farther and farther west.

A quarter of a million people are estimated to have been living in Ephesus in the 1st century CE. At that time the city was at its height as a commercial center and a place of religious pilgrimage for pagans. The occupations of many of the residents were dependent, more or less directly, on the Temple to Diana/Artemis, one of the magnificent architectural wonders of the ancient world. The brisk economic activity associated with this incentive for religious tourism led to the development of banking as we know it.

The temple is represented today by a lonely column in the middle of a swampy field between Ephesus and Selçuk. Very little else is left of it: a few column bases, some fragmented statues, some coins with its picture, and the perplexing 2nd-century CE statues of many-breasted Artemis. The rest is gone—the incense, the excited whispers of the suppliants, the pageantry of the priests, the clamor of the money changers, the statuary, and looming over all the brilliant white marble of the building that could be seen far out to sea.

The ruins of a few other buildings that might have been familiar to Paul stand in Ephesus, some like the Celsus Library, now partially rebuilt by archaeologists. The marble street has been uncovered, and the market place. The theater where the silversmiths denounced Paul has been filled recently to overflowing with audiences acclaiming currently popular international entertainers. As for the tourist trade, it is ironic that the increased interest in the Christian history of Ephesus has generated an increased market in the pagan statues.

As was his wont, Paul began his arguments and persuasions in the synagogue in Ephesus.

> *When some stubbornly refused to believe and spoke evil of the Way before the congregation, he left them, taking the disciples with him, and argued daily in the lecture hall of Tyrannus. This continued for two years, so that all the residents of Asia, both Jews and Greeks, heard the word of the Lord.* (Acts 19:9–10)

The power of Paul's presentation culminated in the protest that was stirred up by the silversmith Demetrius and his craftsmen. Their business had declined because of Paul's denunciation of the worship of false idols, and they judged correctly about the long-term consequences for them:

> *". . . And there is danger not only that this trade of ours may come into disrepute but also that the temple of the great goddess Artemis will be scorned, and she will be deprived of her majesty that brought all Asia and the world to worship her."* (Acts 19:27)

The crowd seized several of Paul's close friends and rushed them into the theater. There for hours they demonstrated, shouting, *"Great is Artemis of the Ephesians!"* (Acts 19:28) By the end of that time most of the people had forgotten what they were there for. Wisely, others of Paul's friends including some of the city officials kept him away. Likewise wisely, the town clerk eventually got there and reminded the crowd that they had legal ways to register their complaints. This assembly, he told them, laid them—not Paul—open to a charge of inciting a riot.

After the disturbance quieted down, Paul said good-by to his friends in Ephesus and left for Macedonia. It would appear that he traveled overland, suggesting that the season was approaching winter. It would also seem reasonable that en route he visited Smyrna (about two days northwest of Ephesus), maybe his friend Lydia's church community in Thyatira (also about two days' travel from Smyrna), and maybe Pergamum (another two days on). These three would later be among the congregations addressed by John in the Book of Revelation.

Miletus

Miletus (Milet) was second to Ephesus as an important city in western Anatolia. A port on the Gulf of Latmus, it was a major mercantile and cultural center from about 1000 BCE into the 4th century CE. Its fortunes fluctuated: Repeatedly it was destroyed and its people killed off by invading Ionians, Lydians, Persians, Macedonians, and, finally, mosquitoes. In between times it prospered mightily. An example of its citizens' wealth and artistic skills, the huge, beautifully carved gate to the market can be seen reconstructed and standing in the Pergamom Museum in Berlin.

The buildings of the well-organized city of Paul's time included the theater, a small temple to Apollo, the gymnasium, the council chamber, a synagogue near the harbor, the market place, the stadium, and the harbor itself. The outlines of these can be traced, along with the statues of two lions that still guard the derelict harbor. The major temple to Apollo 20 kilometers south at Didyma was considered part of the city.

At the end of his last trip through Asia Minor Paul bypassed Ephesus but stopped for several days in Miletus to say good-by to his friends. Sailing from Assos, he stopped briefly on Samos and then went on to Miletus:

> . . . For Paul had decided to sail past Ephesus, so that he might not have to spend time in Asia; he was eager to be in Jerusalem, if possible, on the day of Pentecost.
>
> From Miletus he sent a message to Ephesus, asking the elders of the church to meet him. When they came to him, he said to them: ". . . I do not count my life of any value to myself, if only I may finish my course and the ministry that I received from the Lord Jesus, to testify to the good news of God's grace." . . . When he had finished speaking, he knelt down with them all and prayed. There was much weeping among them all; they embraced Paul and kissed him, grieving especially because of what he had said, that they would not see him again. Then they brought him to the ship. (Acts 20:16–38 passim)

Paul left Miletus believing that he was near the end of his work. He expected, rightly, that he would be persecuted and imprisoned because he had preached God's righteousness as revealed in Jesus Christ.

Paul's Genius

Paul stands within and yet far above his time. So passionate in his cause, so sure that he was wise, but protesting loudly that he was humble—could he have won so many converts without having also set so many against him? In condemning evil, was he without a fault? Or are his shortcomings only those of a genius whose vision has transformed the world?

His understanding of the universe was Aristotelian: *I know a person in Christ who fourteen years ago was caught up to the third heaven . . .* (2 Cor. 12:2)

His acceptance of slavery was Roman: *Slaves, obey your earthly masters in everything, not only while being watched and in order to please them, but wholeheartedly, fearing the Lord.* (Col. 3:22)

His attitude towards women was at times intolerant: *As in all the churches of the saints, women should be silent in the churches. For they are not permitted to speak, but should be subordinate, as the law also says. . . . For it is shameful for a woman to speak in church.* (1 Cor. 14:34–35)

He was an indefatigable worker:

> *But whatever anyone dares to boast of—I am speaking as a fool—I also dare to boast of that. . . . I am a better one: with far greater labors, far more imprisonments, with countless floggings, and often near death. . . . Three times I was shipwrecked; for a night and a day I was adrift at sea; on frequent journeys, in danger from rivers, danger from bandits, danger from my own people, danger from Gentiles, danger in the city, danger in the wilderness, danger at sea, danger from false brothers and sisters; in toil and hardship, through many a sleepless night, hungry and thirsty, often without food, cold and naked. (2 Cor. 11:21–27)*

At the same time he was a cosmopolitan able to move quickly into strange, new situations, a Hebrew scholar able to quote the Bible for any proof of his thesis, and an orator frequently winning converts by his eloquence and conviction. But above all, Paul surpassingly dedicated himself to preaching his vision of the revelation of God as seen in Jesus Christ.

> *If I speak in the tongues of mortals and of angels,*
> *but do not have love, I am a noisy gong or a clanging cymbal.*
> *And if I may have prophetic powers, and understand all mysteries and all knowledge,*
> *And if I have all faith, so as to remove mountains,*
> *but do not have love, I am nothing.*
> *I may give away all my possessions, and if I hand over my body so that I may boast,*
> *but do not have love, I gain nothing.*

Love is patient; love is kind;
love is not envious or boastful or arrogant or rude.
It does not insist on its own way; it is not irritable or
        resentful;
it does not rejoice in wrongdoing, but rejoices in the
        truth.
It bears all things, believes all things, hopes all
things, endures all things.

Love never ends.
But as for prophesies, they will come to an end;
as for tongues, they will cease;
as for knowledge, it will come to an end.
For we know only in part, and we prophesy only in
        part;
but when the complete comes, the partial will come to
        an end.
When I was a child, I spoke like a child,
I thought like a child, I reasoned like a child;
when I became an adult, I put an end to childish ways.
For now we see in a mirror, dimly, but then we will
see face to face.
Now I know only in part;
then I will know fully, even as I have been fully
        known.
And now faith, hope, and love abide, these three;
and the greatest of these is love.

                              1 Corinthians 13

John the Person

John is the named writer of Revelation, the last book of the New Testament. As devoted and intense a missionary as Paul, John's unique contribution to Christianity is his inspired vision. He identified himself at the beginning of this book saying,

> *The revelation of Jesus Christ, which God gave him to show his servants what must soon take place; he made it known by sending his angel to his servant John, who testified to the word of God and to the testimony of Jesus Christ, even to all that he saw.* (Rev. 1:1–2)

Writing to the seven churches in the province of Asia, John called himself a witness (the Greek word is martyr), and his work prophecy. As such, he has long commanded a position of awe with his vision of last things. In its references to existing church communities, the first three chapters of this last book of the Bible are specifically relevant to the early years of Christianity in Anatolia.

Because of John's knowledge of the Old Testament images and liturgy and because of the way he wrote, scholars agree that he was Jewish. Greek probably was not his native language: Those who know biblical Greek point to his many barbarisms. He seems to have been familiar with the letters of Paul and to have quoted phrases from them, but he does not identify them as such. He also seems to have known specific details relevant to each of the Christian congregations in the seven locations that he addressed.

John said that he had been on the island of Patmos in the Aegean because he had been preaching the Christian gospel:

> *I, John, your brother who share with you in Jesus the persecution and the kingdom and the patient endurance, was on the island called Patmos because of the word of God and the testimony of Jesus.* (Rev. 1:9)

This has been taken to mean that he had been sent into exile during the anti-Christian reign of the emperor Domitian (81–96 CE). He said that he had been persecuted. It is also interpreted to imply that he was released when the more tolerant Nerva became emperor. There is no actual proof that this was exile, nor can it be explained—if it was a punishment—why he was exiled rather than executed for the treason of refusing to worship the Roman State. Had the direct question been put to John, surely he would not have temporized.

John said it was on Patmos that he heard a voice telling him to write down what he saw inscribed on a scroll and to send it to the churches. Tradition has added that he had previously been living in Ephesus, and that after his stay on Patmos he returned to Ephesus where he served as its bishop to a ripe old age. According to the 4th-century church historian Eusebius, when he was no longer able to walk, he was carried into the church, saying to all whom he passed on the way, "Little children, love one another."

Church historians do not agree on who John was, when he wrote, or how much he wrote. The first known person to refer to him as the author of Revelation was Justin Martyr, a 2nd-century CE teacher of philosophy. Justin Martyr had been converted to Christianity when he was in Ephesus before 135 CE. He stated specifically that the writer of Revelation was John the apostle, the son of Zebedee. Several other 2nd-century writers, including the highly respected, highly orthodox Irenaeus, accepted the authorship of John the apostle.

The problem began with the 4th-century historian Eusebius who confused rather than contradicted Justin Martyr's assertion by reporting that two Christians named John lived in Ephesus at the same time. Which was who? Next, when the canon of the New Testament books was being considered, other 4th-century churchmen did not want Revelation included. As part of their reasoning for excluding it, they denied that an apostle had written it. Had there not been Justin Martyr's and Irenaeus' attributions of Revelation to the apostle John, it might have been suppressed. The report that John the apostle was martyred in Jerusalem before 70 CE adds to the doubts that John the apostle and the writer of Revelation lived in Ephesus into the end of the 1st century.

There are other points at question: Some have said that the same person wrote not only Revelation but also the Gospel of John and the three letters of John. Others more recently have questioned not only whether the John of Revelation could have written the Gospel account, but also whether the same person wrote all of Revelation. When Justinian built the cathedral over his grave, he dedicated it to "John the

Theologian," an identity that only begs the question. Without firm contemporary evidence, for scholars today the answers to who John was, what, and when he wrote, generally turn on the internal evidence of the language and the ideas in each of the books.

Johannine Traditions

One of the answers to the question of who John was combines the author of the Gospel of John, the author of Revelation, and the beloved friend of Jesus into one person. The tradition held in Ephesus is that John, the author of Revelation, was also the apostle to whom Jesus confided the care of Mary his mother.

Two conflicting traditions concern Mary's activities after Jesus' resurrection. One claim is that she never left Jerusalem. The other is that she came with John to Ephesus. The written evidence for both of these goes back no earlier than the 5th century. The House of Mary (Meryemana) located in the mountains just above Ephesus is believed by many people of many different faiths to have been her last home. Visits here by Pope Paul VI (1967) and Pope John Paul (1979) have conferred an additional public acclaim for this modest, very old stone house.

Certainly the possibility that Mary was in Ephesus adds weight to the supposition that the writer of Revelation was John the beloved disciple. John appears a very human person as he is portrayed by Eusebius in his *Ecclesiastical History*, a person passionate in his convictions and steadfast in his friendships. Eusebius recounts two anecdotes about John that show these qualities. More legend than fact, they lend some color to the realities of his time.

One of them involved John's relationship with a heretic from Egypt by the name of Cerinthus, one of his rivals, who happened to be in Ephesus. Cerinthus taught that the angels made the world, not God, because God could not have made something so imperfect; that Jesus was a man, but that Christ was the Holy Spirit; and that Jesus died, but that Christ ascended into heaven. Each of these teachings would have branded him a heretic in John's eyes, and John would have wanted to distance himself totally from him. Eusebius also charged Cerinthus with discrediting John's authorship of Revelation.

Eusebius repeated the story of John and Cerinthus as the 2nd-century theologian Irenaeus told it in his (lost) book *Against Heresies.* According to the account that Irenaeus had heard from his teacher, Bishop Polycarp of Smyrna, John was enjoying bathing in one of the public baths in Ephesus when he heard Cerinthus' voice as he was entering the building. Seething with annoyance at being caught in his company, John at once leaped up from the bath and fled out into the street, trailing only a small towel of the establishment for cover. "Get out! Quick, get out!" he shouted to his friends inside. "The roof's going to collapse! That enemy of reality will bring everything down on top of us!"

The second story that Eusebius recounted about John has a little more of the ring of authenticity about it. Eusebius prefaced the story with the remark that these events happened during the reign of the emperor Trajan (r. 98–117). He said that John was elderly at the time, and that it was after he had returned from exile on Patmos.

On invitation, John traveled around to various districts, sometimes to install bishops, sometimes to straighten out misunderstandings in the churches. On one of these occasions he found a young man whose bearing and whose personality greatly appealed to him and who he believed would be a credit to the Church. He then commended the youth to the keeping of the bishop of the local church. For some time this bishop looked after the youth, teaching him and at last baptizing him. Believing that with baptism the boy was now safe, the bishop turned him loose and left him to his own devices.

Having too much freedom and too high an opinion of himself, the youth fell in with disreputable companions. First they wined and dined him, then they included him in their misdemeanors. Little by little they led him further into crime until he became himself the leader of a band of brigands, known for banditry and murder.

About then John had reason to revisit the bishop on church business. At the end of their conversation he asked for the return of his investment. The bishop was puzzled about the reference until John said he was interested in seeing the youth whom he had brought him the previous time. With shame, the bishop confessed that he had failed in his responsibility.

"He has died," the bishop said; "he has died to God and taken to the mountains with his gangsters."

Not even changing his clothes, John called for a horse and set out after him alone. Once in the mountains, the brigands easily captured the old man and were about to work their evil on him. Only with difficulty he convinced them that their chief should be the one to decide his fate. As soon as the boy saw him he ran, but John chased him, calling to him that he was still his friend in Christ. The ideal pastor, John stayed with the youth until he had completely repented of his past sins and was restored to faithful membership in the church.

John's Message

Legend or fact, there is little doubt that whoever the John of Revelation was, he wanted and expected to be understood. John fervently desired that the church members receive and heed the message from Jesus Christ that had been revealed to him. His message was of such consequence that John clothed it in the most compelling terms he could command. John knew that the continuance of the Church depended upon the staunch belief of its members, and on their ability to transfer their faith to the next generation. Although today Revelation is considered esoteric, there is also little doubt that John's contemporary audience understood his call to salvation. Perhaps the symbols he used were common within the 1st-century Christian community, but he intentionally clothed his message in the words that carried little force for pagans or the Roman government.

John's writing to the seven churches follows a formal, conventional pattern of salutation, message, warning, and valediction. He begins by greeting the particular congregation: "*to the angel of the church. . .*" Then follows the body of the message with the description of the speaker and his right to speak, with the evidence that he knows the congregation, and with his criticisms and commands. He promises each a distinctive punishment or reward for faithfulness, and concludes with the valediction, *Let anyone who has an ear listen to what the Spirit is saying to the churches.*

People have questioned why John chose these particular churches rather than others nearby. It could have been to illustrate the universal sins that John wanted to highlight: falseness in Ephesus and a faith that cooled, slander in Smyrna, fornication and eating food sacrificed to idols in Pergamum and Thyatira, sloth in Sardis, fraud in Philadelphia, and pride and indifference in Laodicea. Seen from our perspective, these vices appear to foreshadow the seven deadly sins (avarice, sloth, gluttony, lust, wrath, envy, and pride) of the Middle Ages.

In Revelation John was grappling with the consequences of the resurrection. The Good News of Jesus Christ was that all human weaknesses, culminating in death, had been conquered. Therefore death was not to be feared. It was—and is—an exceedingly difficult concept to accept, let alone understand. The message of his vision was so outrageous, so unthinkable, that John couched its transcendence in equally shocking images. But, while he portrayed evil and its horrors, he proclaimed that with faith and steadfastness the final triumph belongs to God.

The Seven Churches of Revelation

John addressed seven church congregations in the first three chapters of Revelation: Ephesus, Smyrna, Pergamum, Thyatira, Sardis, Philadelphia, and Laodicea. He may have sent his message to each of them individually, and then the letters were collected later to be added as a preface to this book of apocalyptic prophesy. Or he may have written expecting that his letter and the accompanying mystical book would be carried on a circuit and each congregation would read and share with others what was addressed to it. He assumed that those who received the message were believers in Christ.

John probably did not intend his message to be confined to the seven; rather he would have counted on its being distributed to the outlying congregations. Scholars believe that the order in which the churches were addressed indicates that these congregations marked an already established path for church-related information that was circulated among them. That there were congregations meeting regularly in each location is obvious, but the number of people in each is not known. It is known, however, from other 2nd-century sources that there were several established churches scattered near this route and in other western Anatolian locations. (At this time people met usually in private homes; buildings specifically dedicated as churches were not built while it was a treasonable offense to practice Christianity openly.)

Revelation is considered to be apocalyptic literature, a particular, artificial, stylized, literary genre that perhaps originated in Mesopotamia with the disappointment of the Jewish exiles. The form concentrates on events leading to the last days; often it has historical details mixed with prophecies about catastrophic upheavals. Supernatural visions, dire judgments, and references understood only by the initiated are common to the genre. For the readers, their unfulfilled expectations, such as the promise of the Second Coming, that were addressed contributed to the popularity of the apocalyptic literature.

Passages in the Old Testament Book of Daniel conform to this genre, as do parts of Isaiah. A number of other pre-Christian writings, among them the *Book of Noah* and the *Apocalypse of Baruch*, fall into this category. In the New Testament, 2nd Thessalonians chapter 2 approaches apocalyptic writing. A 2nd-century CE work, *The Shepherd of Hermas*, was widely read, as was the *Apocalypse of Peter*, to mention only a few.

Like the Old Testament apocalypses, Revelation assumes that the last days will be preceded by a climax of evil, personified by the Antichrist. At the doomsday, God will intervene to judge, condemning the bad to eternal hell and saving the deserving good for heaven, and Christ will come to destroy the Antichrist. Among the references in Revelation that point to Old Testament symbols are the number seven (meaning perhaps completeness, and referring of course to the seven days in which the world was created), Jezebel (who was eaten by dogs as punishment for worshipping Baal), and Balaam (the evil prophet who could not see as well as his donkey).

Ephesus

At the time of John and Paul, Ephesus was at its height in population and prosperity. Many emperors and private citizens had helped embellish it with temples and other public buildings. One of those public buildings was near the old harbor, a basilica that originally was either a part of the harbor facilities or a school. There is no evidence that this was, or was not, the lecture hall of Tyrannus where Paul had taught. By the 3rd century it had been turned into a church. Later at least one other church was added to the original building. In the northeast corner of it is the 4th-century baptistery. In the 5th century two major church councils were held in this building, called the Double Church of the Virgin Mary. The first of those official meetings, known as the Third Ecumenical Council (a most contentious gathering), in 431 condemned the Nestorian heresy. Nestorius was patriarch of Constantinople at the time; his heresy was the denial of the divinity of Jesus. No small amount of the heat in the Council came from a struggle between Constantinople and Rome over primacy, a struggle that eventually culminated in the mutual anathemas pronounced by the Latin (Roman) Catholic Church and the Eastern (Greek) Orthodox Church in 1054. As part of their attempts to heal the rift between East and West, the Catholic Pope Paul VI and the Eastern Orthodox Patriarch Athenagoras lifted the anathemas in 1967. Pope Paul VI that year and Pope John Paul II in 1979 held services in this church.

The city of Ephesus suffered from the silting up of its harbor and the resultant infestation of mosquitoes. By the 6th century most of the residents had moved about a kilometer inland to higher ground to get away from the miasma of the swamp. They took with them many of the dressed stones from the deserted buildings of Ephesus for their new homes. Thus when the emperor Justinian chose to honor the author of Revelation, he built the Cathedral of St. John (using marble taken from Ephesus) on the hill above the new buildings northeast of the old city. In keeping with the custom of the time, the name of this most important church became the name of the new city. Over time, Haghia Theologos (meaning "St. John the Theologian") was softened to Ayasoluk, and then, with the Ottoman Turkish influence, it became Selçuk as it is known today.

John probably died in the early part of the 2nd century. As paganism diminished, pilgrims who had formerly flocked to the temple to Artemis in Ephesus began to visit his grave in

Haghia Theologos. At first there was a wooden church erected over it; this was replaced by Justinian's large marble monument. In the late 20th century people from Lima, Ohio contributed to the partial restoration of Justinian's cathedral. John's grave in this restoration is marked now by a marble slab.

Selçuk is a tourist attraction today not only because of the cathedral and John's grave, but also because of the Ephesus museum that houses frescoes, statues, pottery, and other finds from the region. Several 2nd-century CE representations of Diana/Artemis stand framed by growing ivy. (Other items found by the Austrian archaeologists are displayed in the New Hofburg Museum in Vienna.)

The Book of Revelation begins with the message John heard and which the Angel of the Apocalypse told him to address to seven churches, the first of which was for Ephesus. Perhaps the seven lamps surrounding the Angel that he refers to were reminiscent of lamps at an evening worship service. While some people have thought that the situation that caused him to be on Patmos could have taken place in one of the seven cities, it may be significant that he does not appear to make any specific reference to it or to one of them.

"To the angel of the church in Ephesus write: "These are the words of him who holds the seven stars in his right hand, who walks among the seven golden lampstands:

"I know all your works, your toil and your patient endurance. I know that you cannot tolerate evildoers; you have tested those who claim to be apostles but are not, and have found them to be false. I also know that you are enduring patiently and bearing up for the sake of my name, and that you have not grown weary. But I have this against you, that you have abandoned the love you had at first. Remember then from what you have fallen; repent, and do the works you did at first. If not, I will come to you and remove your lampstand from its place unless you repent. Yet this is to your credit: you hate the works of the Nicolaitans, which I also hate. Let anyone who has an ear listen to what the Spirit is saying to the churches. To everyone who conquers, I will give permission to eat from the tree of life that is in the paradise of God." (Rev. 2:1–7)

Smyrna

Greater Smyrna (Izmir) is wrapped around the east end of a great bay that reaches 75 kilometers east from the Aegean Sea. Itself on gentle slopes, the city is framed by wooded mountains that rise to the east and the south. Among the earliest identified residents are Hittites. Their statuary found in and around Izmir is the best evidence known to date 2nd-millennium BCE Hittite influence this far northwest. The city was a thriving seaport in the 7th century BCE, but had declined to little more than a village when Alexander the Great and his generals revived it in the 4th and 3rd centuries BCE.

The streets of the city founded by Alexander circled the acropolis on Mt. Pagus (Kadifekalesi) which was considered "the crown of Smyrna." The main street was called "Golden"; to use the image of the 2nd-century CE orator Aristedes, the street ran "like a necklace" around the citadel. At its west was a temple to Zeus, and at its east was a temple to the city's goddess, Cybele. The 1st-century CE geographer Strabo considered Smyrna to be the most beautiful city in the Ionia of his time.

Smyrna came under Roman rule in 129 BCE. Columns from the Roman market place are still standing in place; almost unbroken statues of Demeter and Poscidon were uncovered here by 20th-century archaeologists; they are now in the Izmir Archaeological Museum. Other things from the Roman Period are a short stretch of road paralleling Eşref Paşa Caddesi at the top of the hill, and an aqueduct that arches above the Yeşildere Çevre Yolu. Until the 1960s the outlines of the Roman stadium and its tiers of seats could be traced on the west slope of Mt. Pagus, but they have disappeared under today's houses.

There must have been considerable traffic between Ephesus and Smyrna during the years that John and Paul were here. In those days, a person in a hurry could have made the trip overland by horseback in about two days. One could also have gone by sea, but the voyage was considered uphill against the prevailing north wind. A superhighway today spans the 90 kilometers between the two and follows the approximate route those men might have taken.

Smyrna was a commercial rival of Ephesus and Miletus. Smyrna's exports then and now have included figs, raisins, and olive oil. Wine from the Smyrna region was prized by Rome's aristocrats (but they held that it was uncouth to drink it neat; instead they preferred their wines laced with sea water). Well before the 1st century CE, Ephesus and Miletus had to work to keep their harbors open because of their rivers; Smyrna on the other hand never had this problem, as evidenced by its ongoing importance as a major port for Turkey.

A trading center in the Middle Ages, by then Smyrna had become relatively undistinguished. In the late 15th century when Sultan Bayezit II gave the Jewish refugees from the Inquisition in Spain and Portugal hospice in the Ottoman Empire, many of them settled in Smyrna. Within a hundred years their descendents were managing most of the commerce of the empire.

No clear tradition names the founder of the Christian Church in Smyrna, but the records of its bishops begin in the 1st century. Its most famous bishop was the martyred St. Polycarp (c. 63–156 CE), an orphaned slave who, by tradition, was the third to hold that position. In keeping with the other urban centers, probably the first church members were Jews who were part of the large mercantile community. Some of the conflict between the Jews and the Christians, stemming from the immunity the Jews had from Rome in the matter of worshipping the State, is apparent in John's message to the Smyrna congregation.

"And to the angel of the church in Smyrna write: These are the words of the first and the last, who was dead and came to life:

"I know your affliction and your poverty, even though you are rich. I know the slander on the part of those who say they are Jews and are not, but are a synagogue of Satan. Do not fear what you are about to suffer. Beware, the devil is about to throw some of you into prison so you may be tested, and for ten days you will have affliction. Be faithful until death, and I will give you the crown of life. Let anyone who has an ear listen to what the Spirit is saying to the churches. Whoever conquers will not be harmed by the second death." (Rev. 2:8–11)

Pergamum

Pergamum (Bergama) became an important city in the 3rd and 2nd centuries BCE during the rule of the Attalid kings who inherited the northern part of the kingdom created by Alexander the Great. Among them, Eumenes II (r. 197–160 BCE) used his wealth to beautify his capital with such buildings as the temple to Zeus and the theater. Besides supporting the sculptors who created the frieze on the temple, he encouraged the manufacture of parchment (called *pergamena*) that contributed to the enlargement of his library. That library soon rivaled the library in Alexandria, whose citizens considered that theirs was, and always should be, the center of learning.

By 190 BCE the Pergamene kingdom extended through most of western Anatolia as far south as Miletus and as far east as Iconium. Later the Pergamene king Attalus II (160–139 BCE) founded Attalia (Antalya) on the Mediterranean coast in order that his territory of Pamphylia would have a seaport. When the last Attalid king Attalus III (r. 138–133 BCE) willed all his property to Rome, the kingdom was divided into several provinces with the area from Pergamum south to Ephesus becoming the Province of Asia. (At this time the designation of "Asia" was limited to this province; it did not apply to the entire continent.)

The Pergamene acropolis is an impressive site with its main buildings presented so that they would catch the eyes of all who approached it. The hill towers about 400 meters above the plain; on the western slope the spectacular theater rises steeply above the level of the orchestra, providing seating for 10,000 spectators. On the terrace just below the orchestra was a long, colonnaded walkway, a popular place for a promenade, or a conference, or view of the sunset. Above the theater the gleaming white marble temples to Trajan and Hadrian added to the image of the commanding power that the city exercised. These temples have recently regained some of their splendor with the reconstruction work of German and Turkish archaeologists.

Other buildings that must have been there in the 1st century CE are a temple to the kings of Pergamum, a temple to Athena, and next to it the library (Athena was the goddess of wisdom), the gymnasium, a temple to Dionysus (conveniently located at the stage entrance so that the actors could worship their patron god before venturing in front of the audience), the palace, and the market place.

Pergamene grandeur was perhaps best represented in the 2nd-century BCE temple to Zeus, the bare foundations of which are on the southwest edge of the acropolis hill. Two tall pine trees that shade the flat area now add a dimension of height. The largest religious structure in Pergamum, it covered an area about 34 by 36 meters—almost a square. Like a theater, the stepped platform was enclosed on three sides, directing worshippers up the 20 m wide staircase to the central hall and altar. It was unusually squat in proportion to its size. However, in contrast to the Parthenon in Athens (built 300 years earlier), its magnificent frieze for which it is still famous could be admired at eye level rather than soaring at a neck-stretching height above the ground. One of the great masterpieces of Hellenic art, the scenes of the frieze—a battle between the giants and the gods and goddesses—have been interpreted as an intent to show the triumph of Greek civilization in the real battle that the Pergamenes had fought against the Gallic barbarians in 230 BCE. Much of the temple was taken to Berlin in the late 19th century and reconstructed; it is now the showpiece of the Berlin Pergamom Museum in Germany. Visitors to Pergamum in Turkey can see the small copy of it in the Bergama Museum located on the main street of the city.

A monumental red brick building, the Red Basilica, stands to the side of the Selinus (Bergama Çayı) River in modern

Bergama. Probably first a 2nd-century CE structure, archaeologists think it was built for the worship of Serapis. (There
was also a temple to Serapis in Ephesus.) A number of
rooms below ground level accord with the worship of the
Egyptian goddess of the underworld. The original large
courtyard stretched across the present-day street; it was
built over the river which is directed through a large, two-
chambered conduit. The courtyard, once the scene of the
temple ceremony, was later a graveyard; a few tombstones
with Hebrew inscriptions lie off to one side. During the
Byzantine times the central part of the basilica enclosed a
Christian church, of which the floor is still left. One of the
two towers of the temple has been converted into a
mosque.

Not far from the acropolis of Pergamum, and at one of the
many thermal springs of the region, was one of the region's
most popular medical centers, the Asclepion. Named for
Asclepius, the god of medicine, the center was as much a
place of worship as of healing. Now largely excavated, the
area covered a rectangular courtyard with a small theater
facing into it on the northwest side. Doctors' offices and
their homes were located just beyond the theater. During
the 2nd century CE, Galen, the doctor whose writings above
all others influenced medical practice for centuries, was in
residence here. Galen was grounded in Stoic philosophy,
and therefore based his work on the premise that God created everything to serve a purpose. His practical medicine
was directed to aiding the diagnosis of a disease. Galen's
writings were lost to Europe until they were rediscovered in

their Arabic translation by Maimonides and the Crusaders in the 12th century. (Maimonides was personal physician to Saladin, the Kurdish sultan of Egypt, and accompanied him on his conquests.)

While most of the buildings now visible (the circular treatment room with six apses, the tunnel running to the treatment room, the temple to Asclepius, and the colonnades) were built after the 1st century CE, the central well would have always been the focus of the complex. Water from that well was used for drinking and bathing. Water from another well created the mud in which the patients immersed themselves to be healed of their skin diseases.

In the valley between the acropolis and the Asclepion are the ruins of a Roman amphitheater—a theater with the orchestra/stage completely surrounded by banks of seats for the spectators. This one made use of the stream over which it is located; when the entertainment demanded it, the stream was dammed to flood the orchestra in order for the performers to stage mock naval battles. Also, gladiator fights being frequent amusements for the Romans, one might imagine more than one Christian facing a lion, or a bear, or maybe a crocodile here.

Biblical scholars have speculated that, because the temple to Zeus so defined the Pergamene scene, it was the throne of Satan to which John referred. Another interpretation has been that Satan's throne was a reference to the Roman government because of the persecutions that Christians in Pergamum were experiencing.

"And to the angel of the church in Pergamum write: These are the words of him who has the sharp two-edged sword: "I know where you are living, where Satan's throne is. Yet you are holding fast to my name, and you did not deny your faith in me even in the days of Antipas my faithful witness, my faithful one, who was killed among you, where Satan lives. But I have a few things against you: you have some there who hold to the teaching of Balaam, who taught Balak to put a stumbling block before the people of Israel, so that they would eat food sacrificed to idols and practice fornication. So you also have some who hold the teaching of the Nicolaitans. Repent then. If not, I will come to you soon and make war against them with the sword of my mouth. Let anyone who has an ear listen to what the Spirit is saying to the churches. To everyone who conquers I will give some of the hidden manna, and I will give a white stone, and on the stone is written a new name that no one knows except the one who receives it." (Rev. 2:12–17)

Thyatira

The history of Thyatira (Akhisar) is of little interest to those other than church historians, and is little noted in guidebooks or in the history of Asia Minor. Its records show no great men, no famous buildings, no major battles. A quietly prosperous agricultural city with grapes and cotton its main commodities, it lies in the fertile valley of the Lycus (Kum Çayı) River, a tributary of the Hermus (Gediz) River.

Thyatira was founded by the Lydians in the 6th century BCE around the time that Croesus was king and controlled this general area. Two centuries later Seleucis 1 Nicator contributed to its city finances and moved his soldiers here from Macedonia in order to defend it against his rival, Lysimachus, the ruler of the Pergamenes. Seleucis is reported by the 1st-century CE Jewish historian Josephus to have rewarded Jewish residents of the cities that he supported with citizenship. Thyatira was on the Imperial Post Road—the road maintained by Rome to keep communications open between the capital and its provinces. It continues to be a stopping point on a major commercial route linking Izmir and Istanbul.

Of the cities in the province of Asia, Thyatira had the greatest variety of registered trade guilds, among them coppersmiths, weavers, and potters. One of the symbols found on coins of the city was of the god Tyrimnos; the Greek equivalent of this god was Hephestus, the lame god of fire. On a coin of the city he is dressed as a smith and is holding a bronze helmet that he was finishing for Pallas Athena. This is cited as part of the evidence that indicates that John knew and used local symbolism in his letter when he spoke of burnished bronze for Thyatira. But the actual prophetess Jezebel of Thyatira whom John condemned to a bed of pain has been lost to history.

The ancient buildings now easily visible in Thyatira/Akhisar are concentrated within a city block. They include a basilica (probably once the city court house) and the fallen arches that marked the colonnaded market street. Thyatira was the home of Lydia, the seller of purple goods whom Paul had converted on his first visit to Philippi. John's address shows that the Christian community there was active; at the same time its members provoked the longest of his remarks.

"And to the angel of the church in Thyatira write: These are the words of the Son of God, who has eyes like a flame of fire and whose feet are like burnished bronze.

"I know your works—your love, faith, and patient endurance. I know that your last works are greater than the first. But I have this against you: you tolerate that woman Jezebel, who calls herself a prophet and is teaching and beguiling my servants to practice fornication and to eat food sacrificed to idols. I gave her time to repent, but she refuses to repent of her fornication. Beware, I am throwing her on a bed and those who commit adultery with her I am throwing into great distress, unless they repent of her doings; and I will strike her children dead. And all the churches will know that I am the one who searches minds and hearts, and I will give to each of you as your works deserve. But to the rest of you in Thyatira, who do not hold this teaching, who have not learned what some call the deep things of Satan, to you I say, I do not lay on you any other burden; only hold fast to what you have until I come. To everyone who conquers and continues to do my works to the end,

I will give authority over the nations;
to rule them with an iron rod,
as when clay pots are shattered—

even as I also received authority from my Father. To the one who conquers I will also give the morning star. Let anyone who has an ear listen to what the Spirit is saying to the churches." (Rev. 2:18–29)

Sardis

The history of Sardis (Sart), the ancient capital of Lydia, began long before the Christian era. Perhaps the first reference to the people of Sardis is in the listing of Noah's descendants: Lud is presumed to be the progenitor of the Lydians. Other Old Testament references, direct or indirect, include the 9th-century BCE Cimmerians or Scythians (again supposed descendants of Noah through Japheth) who invaded and captured Sardis. The book of the prophet Obadiah has reference to Sepharad (*the exiles of Jerusalem who are in Sepharad shall possess the towns of the Negeb*), identified by biblical scholars as Sardis. The exiles there could have been 6th-century BCE Jewish refugees (Obad. 20) or prisoners of war sold as slaves to the people of Sardis.

Through the writings of Greek historians (notably Herodotus) and through stone inscriptions, the major happenings in Sardis are chronicled from about the 7th century BCE. One of the early kings, Gyges (c. 680–652 BCE), was mentioned by the Assyrian king Assurpanipal. A later king Croesus and his fabler Aesop are household names more than 2500 years after their deaths. One story not told by Aesop is that, rather than getting his wealth by panning for gold in the small stream flowing through Sardis, Croesus stretched sheepskins across the stream and thus trapped the nuggets. Perhaps this is the origin of the idea of the Golden Fleece.

Under Croesus, Sardis was the capital of the Lydian kingdom. By his time its citizens had made several enduring contributions to western society: They had aided the development of commerce by minting coins of a standard weight and content and by guaranteeing their value. Their musicians had added an extra string to their lyres. They had invented dice by adding markings (and sometimes unequal weights) to the knobby backbones that their gamesters rolled.

But then, misreading the advice of an oracle, Croesus pitted his empire against the Persian rule of Cyrus the Great. Croesus lost. The deathblow came when soldiers on the Sardis citadel were careless in their guard and Cyrus's men stole in as thieves in the night. With this, Sardis became a Persian satrapy in 546 BCE, and thus the western center of the Persian empire. The balance of power tipped east away from the Mediterranean, and much of the traffic then coursed over the main Royal Road between Sardis and Susa. Even so, probably not much changed for the man in the street whose language continued to be Greek.

The next political change came with Alexander the Great in 333 BCE when he set out through Anatolia determined to conquer his world and to impose Greek culture on it. His control in Sardis was followed by the Seleucid Empire, and then in 133 BCE Rome took over.

The ruined temple to Artemis at Sardis is one of the most impressive ancient buildings still visible in Asia Minor. Apparently there was a previous temple to the Anatolian Cybele here dating from the 5th century BCE. When Alexander arrived in Sardis, he ordered that the worship be changed to the Greek goddess of the Moon and of the hunt. These modifications held into the Christian era, until in the 4th century CE paganism was outlawed. A small Byzantine period church in ruins now huddles in the southeast corner. The temple and the city have suffered badly from a number of earthquakes, and from the ravages of Tamerlane in the early 15th century.

Near the stream and the modern highway archaeologists have discovered the ancient gold refinery dating from the time of Croesus. Also in that area are the ruins of an early Christian church.

Besides the temple, two other buildings are stately examples of their time: The partially reconstructed 3rd-century CE gymnasium and synagogue are located adjacent to the main Izmir-Ankara highway. At the time the gymnasium was built it was more a place where men met for mental exercise than for physical, but there was also a wrestling school connected with the gym, and a large bath-pool. The partially reconstructed synagogue, a beautiful building recently decorated with patterned marble, was begun in the 3rd century CE and repaired later in the 4th. The walls of the small shops that back up against the synagogue are likewise early Byzantine in date.

The theater, a 1st-century CE building, can be traced on a bowl on the north slope of the citadel hill. It overlooks the ruins of the Roman stadium.

According to Herodotus, in an attempt to rescue his fellow Lydians from slavery, Croesus bargained with his captor, Cyrus. Croesus secured their freedom by promising that, instead of being trained as warriors and bearing arms, all the sons would be shopkeepers and learn to play musical instruments. From then on they and their neighbors the Phrygians were considered lazy and effeminate.

In John's vision, he was less concerned with their effeminacy than that they were unprepared and still lazy.

> *"And to the angel of the church in Sardis write: These are the words of him who has the seven spirits of God and the seven stars.*
>
> *"I know your works; you have a name of being alive, but you are dead. Wake up, and strengthen what remains and is on the point of death, for I have not found your works perfect in the sight of my God. Remember then what you received and heard; obey it, and repent. If you do not wake up, I will come like a thief, and you will not know at what hour I will come to you. Yet you have still a few persons in Sardis who have not soiled their clothes; they will walk with me, dressed in white, for they are worthy. If you conquer, you will be clothed like them in white robes, and I will not blot your name out of the book of life; I will confess your name before my Father and before his angels. Let anyone who has an ear listen to what the Spirit is saying to the churches."* (Rev. 3:1–6)

Philadelphia

Attalus II of Pergamum chose the name "Philadelphia" (brotherly love) for the military border post on the eastern edge of the Pergamene kingdom in order to commemorate the close friendship between him and his brother Eumenes II. Philadelphia (Alaşehir) was founded about 150 BCE as a kind of door between Pergamum and Galatia with its strategic location on the main trade route from Sardis to Susa. It is on the plain of the Hermus (Gediz) River just at the point that the road starts up the northern slope of the Tmolus (Bozdağ) Mountains. Philadelphia grew to be a cultural as well as a military center for the region, and was known as "Little Athens" because of its temples and all the public festivals celebrated there.

Of the buildings that might have been important during the Roman period, very little is visible now in the city. Much of the reason for this is that it has suffered frequently and heavily from tectonic activity. The city has suffered from human violence also: That scourge Tamerlane captured it in 1402 and built a wall with the bodies of its residents.

The site of the Roman theater on the hillside in Alaşehir has been uncovered showing a few of the stones of the seats. Farther up, part of the citadel wall is a reminder of the military character of the old city. Physical evidence of Christianity in Philadelphia can be seen in the remains of an 11th-century basilical church. Other than that, the name is preserved in the title of the Greek Orthodox Archbishop of Philadelphia, and in the name of a city in the United States.

John's attention was apparently drawn to the facts that Philadelphia was a border post and that its Christian congregation was small:

> "And to the angel of the church at Philadelphia write:
>   These are the words of the holy one, the true one,
>   who has the key of David,
>   who opens and no one may shut,
>   who shuts and no one opens:

> "I know your works. Look, I have set before you an open door, which no one is able to shut. I know that you have but little power, and yet you have kept my word and have not denied my name. I will make those of the synagogue of Satan who say that they are Jews and are not, but are lying—I will make them come and bow down before your feet, and they will learn that I have loved you. Because you have kept my word of patient endurance, I will keep you from the hour of trial that is coming on the whole world to test the inhabitants of the earth. I am coming soon; hold fast what you have, so that no one may seize your crown. If you conquer, I will make you a pillar in the temple of my God; you will never go out of it. I will write on you the name of my God, and the name of the city of my God, the new Jerusalem that comes down from my God out of heaven, and my own new name. Let anyone who has an ear listen to what the Spirit is saying to the churches." (Rev. 3:7–13)

Laodicea

Located at a major crossroads, Laodicea (Laodikya) was an important banking and manufacturing city. It lay about equidistance between Hierapolis to the north and Colossae to the southeast. The wool industry seems to have helped make Laodicea famous; its cloth called *colossinus* was known far and wide for its softness and its lustrous black color.

Laodicea had its own medical institution dedicated to the god Men-Karou; its physicians worked on the principle that a disease that had compound symptoms needed compound medicine. The Pergamene doctor Galen prescribed a number of herbs to heal his patients, among them spikenard. This was a medicinal herb that came from Laodicea that he may have used to treat eye diseases. The ointment for the Laodiceans' eyes that John prescribed could be his way of connecting his warning with their well-known medicine.

A decision by Rome in 62 BCE to confiscate the yearly tribute (over twenty pounds of gold) that the Jews of Laodicea were in the habit of sending to Jerusalem is evidence that they were a significant community there. However, Rome was not always oppressive: In 40 BCE, in gratitude for the Laodiceans having resisted the revolt led by Labienus after Julius Caesar was assassinated, Mark Anthony made a number of its residents Roman citizens.

Laodicea has not been fully excavated, nor has what has been found been judged to be of particular value. Therefore, its rather flat hilltop does not attract a long visit by most people. There is a stadium and next to it what was perhaps a bath or gymnasium. The public fountain, ruins of several unidentified buildings, the aqueduct, and two theaters can be seen concealed in the early summer by wheat growing among the scattered stones.

Situated in a fertile, well-watered valley, two of Laodicea's neighbors were also biblically important cities. Hierapolis, known today for its "cotton castle" (Pamukkale) of white terraced travertine pools, was a spa and probably retirement center in the 1st century CE. The apostle Philip is said to have lived here in his later years. Scholars have speculated that its springs of hot water may have occasioned John's reference to Laodicea across the valley being only lukewarm. The other city, Colossae, was both the home of Paul's friends Philemon and Onesimus and the object of his letter to the Colossians. Both Laodicea and Hierapolis are named several times in Colossians.

John's address to the Laodiceans is both directed to them and seems to sum up his message to all the churches:

"And to the angel of the church in Laodicea write: The words of the Amen, the faithful and true witness, the origin of God's creation:

"I know your works; you are neither cold nor hot. I wish that you were either cold or hot. So, because you are lukewarm, and neither cold nor hot, I am about to spit you out of my mouth. For you say, 'I am rich, I have prospered, and I need nothing.' You do not realize that you are wretched, pitiable, poor, blind, and naked.

Therefore I counsel you to buy from me gold refined by fire so that you may be rich; and white robes to clothe you and to keep the shame of your nakedness from being seen; and salve to anoint your eyes so that you may see."

The end of the chapter could be read as a summation of John's message, and thus seen to be addressed to the members of all the churches:

I reprove and discipline those whom I love. Be earnest, therefore, and repent. Listen! I am standing at the door, knocking; if you hear my voice and open the door, I will come in to you and eat with you, and you with me. To the one who conquers I will give a place with me on my throne, just as I myself conquered and sat down with my Father on his throne. Let anyone who has an ear listen to what the Spirit is saying to the churches." (Rev. 3:14–22)

Revelation continues, after John's vision of the evil violence and destruction of Armageddon, to his prophesy of a new heaven, a new earth, and a holy city—the new Jerusalem.

Anatolian Church Fathers

Paul and John wrote expecting that the kingdom of God was at hand. They were concerned to prepare everyone they could for the final test that would determine who was saved and who was damned. By the 2nd century, however, Christians were no longer certain of a decisive and immediate

Armageddon. They were caught in the realities of ongoing, humdrum life, and with the Roman government's decision that their refusal to worship the State was treason.

It was a time when many were wrestling with what of this new faith to believe, who of its preachers to listen to, and how much latitude should be allowed in the interpretations. The discussions (debates, arguments) engaged everyone. By the 4th century, Bishop Gregory of Nazianzus, who had been trying to control the meeting of the Second Ecumenical Council, said that the council members sounded like scolding magpies. Bishop Gregory of Nyssa grumbled that when he had asked the maid if she had gotten his bath ready she told him that the Son had been gotten out of nothing. With these came the questions and power struggles over who should make the decision, the Bishop of Rome, or the Bishop of Jerusalem, the Emperor, or the street cleaner. Obviously by this time, no one had a personal acquaintance with Jesus or his apostles, but rather relied on the few written accounts and their various interpretations.

Two 2nd-century leaders illustrate opposing responses to what they believed was demanded of them by their faith. Ignatius (d. c. 110 CE) apparently had been converted in a sudden and wrenching event. When challenged by the Roman government, he welcomed his tribulation and rushed to meet his judgment as one possessed. His contemporary Polycarp (c. 70–156 CE), a Christian from childhood, faced his trial deliberately. Both were equal in their commitment to the faith, both were pivotal in the development of the Church; both have emulators even today.

The small body of their writings has been preserved to justify the historical authenticity of certain beliefs and practices. As one example, because the 2nd-century heretic Marcion based so much of his doctrine on quotations from Paul's letters, the 4th-century churchmen attempted to discredit everything that Paul wrote. Polycarp's recommendation was enough that in the end Paul's work was accepted as part of the New Testament canon. Both Ignatius and Polycarp died for their faith, Ignatius probably in Rome as a gladiator, Polycarp at the stake in Smyrna.

Ignatius

Ignatius was the second bishop after Peter of the church in Antioch. There is no evidence other than his probable age (60?, 70?) that he knew any of the first Antiochene Christians. His importance is because of seven letters he wrote about Christian practices; these came to be used to define orthodoxy. En route to Rome for trial and presumed martyrdom, he stopped in Smyrna about 110. There Bishop Polycarp hosted him, and while there Christian leaders of the area took the occasion to meet him.

Like Paul on his journey to Rome, Ignatius was in the charge of a body of soldiers whom he called leopards. The image of leopards implies that he thought he was being treated harshly. It may well have been so, but again, in those years a man took his life in his hands if he traveled alone.

Almost nothing personal about him appears in his letters. His writing suggests that he was a sensitive, high strung, overzealous individual. Writing to the Roman Christians, he said, *Let me be given to the wild beasts, for through them I can attain unto God. I am God's wheat, and I am ground by the wild beasts that I may be found the pure bread of Christ.*

Besides glorying in martyrdom, Ignatius was fervent in denouncing what he considered the heresy that denied the humanity of Christ. He urged the Church to maintain its unity, and stressed the absolute authority of the bishop over his flock.

Polycarp

Polycarp, too, was a martyr, but in contrast to Ignatius, he was not a fanatic. Since he knew John in Ephesus, he is counted the direct link between the apostolic tradition and the early Church theologians.

Polycarp was born a Christian rather than winning his faith through hardship or blinding revelation. He became a church leader because of his skills in helping and healing, because of his good sense in dealing with people, and because of his own self-discipline. He grew in his encounter with Ignatius whom he respected but did not emulate. He took on added responsibilities in church affairs outside his local community after that encounter.

As the representative of the Eastern Churches, he went to Rome in about 155 to discuss points of practice concerning the celebration of the crucifixion and Easter. By his own account, he was at least 85 years old at the time. There he faced the challenge of divergent opinions and won both a compromise and the respect of the leaders in the West.

With this increased international standing, he returned to his duties in Smyrna. Shortly thereafter he was brought to trial before the Roman provincial governor who tried to save him from an angry crowd. When the governor offered him a simple statement supporting Rome, Polycarp turned on him saying stoutly, "Don't pretend you don't know who I am. I cannot worship your pagan gods. I will not be guilty of blasphemy. I am a Christian."

Polycarp and his period have many parallels with people and events today. He lived at a time in which the standards of society were being threatened by the explosion of knowledge and communication, and by the breakdown of conventional religious practices, a time when the coarseness in language was acceptable and brutality was entertainment. It was one when force and terror were being used for political and religious purposes. It was also a time in which many were confidently—and fearfully—looking forward to the imminent end of the world.

Polycarp was not a great theologian or a profound writer, but he distinguished clearly between exploiting the personal and political power he could command and sacrificing himself to save others, between creating terror to forward his cause and standing for his cause in spite of fear, and between using his life for self-advancement and being used by God. By his death he was lifted out of obscurity to set a standard of integrity for all who have witnessed to God's redemptive majesty.

THE SETTINGS AND THE SEERS

The geographic settings of biblical images begin in eastern Turkey with the vision of a paradise between the two rivers; they end on the western coast with churches immortalized in a revelation. A shipbuilder talking with God, a shepherd called to found a nation, a prophet knocking on doors—over and over the people of this land have envisioned insights that have addressed the questions of how God works in human life. Each insight has been as unique as the person who spoke; each has added to the collected wisdom of their age. Nor have their answers all been gentle. Natural disasters such as floods are interlaced in the account with petty personal jealousies and overwhelmingly hideous wars. The humans through whom the questions and answers have come have been fallible. From Cain's agonizing cry, "Am I my brother's keeper?" to Peter's denial of his Lord, the images have defined the cost of goodness. With them God has spoken through human agents to accomplish His will.

The legacy of these prophets is their inspired concept of God passed on to us in scripture. They have tried to make immediate their insights into how the grace of God works in our lives. In picture and poetry and prophecy, in homely parable and thundering sermon they have spoken, in spite of contempt and martyrdom. The Flood and the rainbow, the morning star and the lukewarm follower spewed out of God's mouth, the nomad and the missionary walking step by step across the land still stir our recognition of God's majesty and glory and command a humility in the awe with which we worship God. In touching what is beyond the words, the prophets' visions continue to challenge us to accept and make real God's commands to love God with all our hearts and minds and souls and to love our neighbors as ourselves. Perhaps the broken relation between us sinners and perfect God, symbolized in the parable of Adam and Eve, has driven our restless search for human salvation.

Over the centuries, and to a degree only less than the land of Palestine, Anatolia has figured in the setting of the biblical events and parables. Abraham walked this land, and maybe the Virgin Mary. Paul, who was an accomplice in the stoning of Stephen, and Peter, who denied Christ, carried their perceptions here, along with doubting Thomas. These, and many more named and unnamed saints and sinners who lived here, have empowered others with visions that have transformed Judaism and Christianity.

The revelations have gone on beyond these people of the Bible. Much of later Christian history also centered in Turkey. Bishop Polycarp of Smyrna dedicated his life that others might know through him God's grace. The theologians of the Ecumenical Councils, the builders of St. Sophia, and the artists of St. Savior in Chora gave their hearts and minds to creating expressions of wonder, awe, and praise for God. We who walk here now as pilgrims searching for answers to our relationships with God share these symbols. We find in them not only our past but also our wholeness. In touching what is beyond words, the visionaries have challenged us to see what they have seen, and hear within ourselves what they have heard.

ACKNOWLEDGMENTS

This book has developed out of the experiences and insights that the author has gained through her writing of *Biblical Sites in Turkey* (co-author Everett C. Blake, SEV-Yay, Istanbul) and *Turkey's Religious Sites* (DAMKO, Istanbul). Along with these have been the frequent visits she has been privileged to make over the course of fifty years to the places described here. As with those books, many, many thanks are owed to many people over many years for its preparation. Obviously, the primary reference has been the Bible. The works of archaeologists in Turkey and biblical scholars make up another body of important source materials. These are noted formally in the Suggested Readings. The author also thanks her editor, Dr. Brian Johnson, and staff of Archaeology and Art Publications for their technical help. The libraries of the American Board in Istanbul and the American Research Institute of Turkey have been invaluable resources. She is grateful for the early advice and admonition of the Drs. Paul and Gladys Minear who added their skilled biblical and editorial wisdom. The help of friends mentioned in the previous books has continued to be relevant, as have the comments of those who have read those books. Again at each of the sites there have been museum directors, guides, workers, and school children who have given their interpretations and color to her understanding. Above all these, however, have been the meticulous editing of her son James and the tireless, multifaceted support of her husband William. But in the end, the responsibility for what is written lies solely with the author. To all of these, and to the people of Turkey she dedicates this book, hoping that it may stimulate others to value this Holy Land.

Istanbul, July 2002

SUGGESTED READINGS

Adeney, Walter F., *The Greek and Eastern Churches*, The International Theological Library, Charles Scribner's Sons, New York, 1908

Aksit, Ilhan, *Ancient Civilizations of Anatolia and Historical Treasures of Turkey*, Ali Rıza Başkan—Güzel Sanatlar Matbaası A.Ş., Istanbul, 1982

Akurgal, Ekrem, *Ancient Civilizations and Ruins of Turkey*, Hacet Kitapevi, Istanbul, 1985

Blake, Everett C., and Edmonds, Anna G., *Biblical Sites in Turkey*, SEV-Yay, Istanbul, 1998

Cumont, Franz, *The Oriental Religions in Roman Paganism*, Dover Publications, New York, 1956

Dio Cassius, *Dio's Roman History*, trans. Ernest Cary, vols. II, VI, Loeb Classical Library, 1968

Edmonds, Anna G., *Turkey's Religious Sites*, DAMKO, Istanbul, 1997

Eerdman's Handbook to the Bible, Eerdmans, Grand Rapids, MI, 1992

Encyclopedia Britannica, Eleventh Edition, vols. 1–28, Encyclopedia Britannica Inc., New York, 1911

Eusebius, *Ecclesiastical History*, Catholic University of America, Washington, 1953

Foss, Clive, *Ephesus After Antiquity*, Cambridge University Press, 1979

Harper's Bible Dictionary, Harper & Row, Publishers, San Francisco, 1985

Joukowsky, Martha Sharp, *Early Turkey, An Introduction to the Archaeology of Anatolia from Prehistory through the Lydian Period*, Kendall Hunt Publishing Company, Dubuque, Iowa, 1996

Keller, Werner, *The Bible as History*, Morrow, New York, 1981

Koester, Helmut, *Ephesos Metropolis of Asia: an interdisciplinary Approach to Its Archaeology*, Trinity Press International, Valley Forge, Pa, 1995

Lawrence, D. H., (Kalnins, Mara, ed.,) *Apocalypse and the Writings on Revelation*, Cambridge University Press, 1980

MacDonald, Dennis Ronald, *The Legend and the Apostle: the Battle for Paul in Story and Canon*, Westminster Press, 1983

New English Bible, 2nd ed., Oxford and Cambridge University Presses, Oxford, 1970

Minear, Paul S., *I Saw a New Earth: An Introduction to the Visions of the Apocalypse*, Corpus, Washington, 1968

--, *New Testament Apocalyptic*, Abingdon, Nashville, 1981

Pagels, Elaine, *The Gnostic Gospels*, Random House, New York, 1979

Ramsay, W. M., *The Historical Geography of Asia Minor*; Royal Geographical Society Supplementary Papers, Vol. IV; London, John Murray, 1890

--, *The Cities of St. Paul*, Baker Book House, Grand Rapids, MI, 1963

--, *The Letters to the Seven Churches of Asia*, Hodder and Stoughton, London, 1904

Schaff, Philip, and Wace, Henry, eds., *A Select Library of Nicene and Post-Nicene Fathers of the Christian Church*, Second Series, The Christian Literature Company, New York, 1895

Schüssler-Fiorenza, Elisabeth, *In Memory of Her*, Crossroad, New York, 1987

--, *The Book of Revelation, Justice and Judgment*, Fortress Press, Philadelphia, 1985

Seval, Mehlika, *Let's Visit Ephesus*, Mas Matbaacılık A.Ş., Istanbul, n.d.

Stanley, Arthur Penrhyn, *Lectures on the History of the Eastern Church*, John Murray, London, 1908

Streete, Gail P., *Her Image of Salvation: Female Saviors and Formative Christianity*, Westminster/John Knox Press, 1992

Taşlılan, Mehmet, Pisidian Antioch, "*The Journeys of St. Paul to Antioch*", Göltaş Cultural Series 2, Ankara, 1997

Thompson, Leonard L., *The Book of Revelation, Apocalypse and Empire*, Oxford University Press, 1990

Torrey, Charles Cutler, *The Apocryphal Literature, a Brief Introduction*, Yale University Press, 1945

--, *VII. Müze Kurtarma Kazıları Semineri, 8-10 Nisan 1996*, Kuşadası-Aydın, Ankara, 1997

Underwood, Paul A., *The Kariye Djami, Vol. I, Historical Introduction and Description of the Mosaics and Frescoes*, Bollingen Series LXX, Pantheon Books, 1966